12 Characteristics of Deliberate Homework

Learn how to assign homework that truly enhances learning and isn't just busywork. This important book defines what deliberate homework looks like and provides relevant, actionable suggestions to guide your homework decisions. You'll uncover how to think through these 12 characteristics of homework:

- ◆ reasonable completion time
- ◆ the right level of complexity
- ◆ appropriate frequency
- ◆ serves a specific purpose
- ◆ aligns with learning targets
- ◆ guided by a learning mindset
- ◆ contains a thoughtful format
- ◆ fits the learning sequence
- ◆ communicated clearly
- ◆ followed by feedback
- ◆ uses grades to guide progress
- ◆ implementation is consistent

For each feature, the author includes strategies and tools appropriate for all grade levels. The book also includes self-assessments and reflective questions so you can work on the book independently or with colleagues in professional development sessions.

Erik Youngman has been in educational leadership for more than 19 years. He is the Director of Curriculum, Instruction, and Assessment for Libertyville District 70 in Libertyville, Illinois. Previously, he served as a principal in Libertyville as well as an assistant principal and teacher in Gurnee, Illinois. You can connect with him via Twitter: @Erik_Youngman.

T0373582

Also Available from Routledge
Eye On Education
(www.routledge.com/k-12)

10 Perspectives on Learning in Education
Edited by Jimmy Casas, Todd Whitaker, Jeff Zoul

10 Perspectives on Innovation in Education
Edited by Jimmy Casas, Todd Whitaker, Jeff Zoul

**What Great Teachers Do Differently, 2nd Edition:
17 Things That Matter Most**
Todd Whitaker

**What Great Principals Do Differently, 2nd Edition:
18 Things That Matter Most**
Todd Whitaker

Your First Year: How to Survive and Thrive as a New Teacher
Todd Whitaker, Madeline Whitaker Good, Katherine Whitaker

Classroom Management from the Ground Up
Todd Whitaker, Madeline Whitaker Good, Katherine Whitaker

10 Keys to Student Empowerment: Unlocking the Hero in Each Child
Cathleen Beachboard and Marynn Dause

**Working Hard, Working Happy: Cultivating a Culture of Effort
and Joy in the Classroom**
Rita Platt

12 Characteristics of Deliberate Homework

Erik Youngman

Routledge
Taylor & Francis Group

NEW YORK AND LONDON

First published 2020
by Routledge
52 Vanderbilt Avenue, New York, NY 10017

and by Routledge
2 Park Square, Milton Park, Abingdon, Oxon, OX14 4RN

Routledge is an imprint of the Taylor & Francis Group, an informa business

© 2020 Taylor & Francis

Library of Congress Cataloging-in-Publication Data
A catalog record for this title has been requested

ISBN: 978-0-367-43312-3 (hbk)
ISBN: 978-0-367-43311-6 (pbk)
ISBN: 978-1-003-00241-3 (ebk)

Typeset in Palatino
by SPi Technologies India Private Limited

Contents

Figures

Tables

Meet the Author

Erik Youngman is an education leader who is passionate about topics such as homework, grading, leadership, and growth mindset. He recently completed his 19th year in educational leadership. Erik is the Director of Curriculum, Instruction, and Assessment for Libertyville District 70 in Libertyville, Illinois. Previous education experiences include being a principal in Libertyville as well as an assistant principal and teacher in Gurnee, Illinois.

Erik earned a Doctorate in Educational Leadership, an Education Specialist Degree, and a Master of Science in Education from Northern Illinois University and a Bachelor of Arts from Augustana College. Please follow and contact Erik via Twitter: @Erik_Youngman.

Acknowledgments

This book is dedicated to my family and educators. I am grateful for the inspiration, encouragement, and support from my wife, Amber; my three daughters, Anika, Tessa, and Fiona; my brothers, Paul, John, Jesse, and Tony; and my parents, Bob and Laila Youngman. I appreciate their positive impact on my collective values for learning, athletics, fine arts, and family.

I want to express gratitude to the educators who empowered my passion for learning at Racine Unified School District, Augustana College, and Northern Illinois University, especially Gail Jacky for her writing support. Finally, I want to thank educators and authors Cathy Vatterott and Jeff Zoul for making time to discuss education topics with me and inspiring me to share my learning with teachers, administrators, and parents.

Introduction

Homework continues to be a relevant topic that parents and educators typically have opinions about. Homework discussion topics can range from the difficulty level, equity, and completion time to banning or mandating homework. Not assigning homework potentially limits practice, extension, or review opportunities, while mandated nightly homework can be burdensome and/or busy work. My experiences as a teacher, assistant principal, principal, curriculum director, and father have guided me to believe that reasonable, meaningful, informative, and consistent homework should be the goal rather than banning it or mandating nightly homework minutes. Rather than assigning daily homework that is a stressful busywork obligation, empowering students with reasonable, meaningful, informative, and consistent homework can inspire ownership, curiosity, innovation, or reflection to ultimately ignite a love for continuous learning.

A primary goal for education is to inspire students to be lifelong learners. Teachers who empower and engage their students motivate them to want to learn. Thus, the following homework recommendations can guide school districts to empower a continuous learning mindset that ignites curiosity and interest rather than extinguishing interest and confidence. If you assign homework, the characteristics and questions in this book should guide your decisions.

The purpose of this book is to simplify the complex topic of homework by asking deliberate questions to empower reflection, discussion, and meaningful homework practices. This book is based on the following premises. Homework can be thought of as independent practice. Regardless of whether this happens at home as homework or at the beginning, during, or end of class, practice can be enhanced by reflecting on the guidelines in this book. Homework should enhance understanding and proficiency while building students' academic success and confidence in the classroom. Homework should be timely and productive, align with effective teaching and learning practices, and support or enhance learning.

This book explores relevant and actionable suggestions to guide homework decisions by defining the structure of deliberate homework. "Deliberate homework" is defined in this book as intentionally planned purposeful school work completed outside of the classroom that is reasonable, meaningful, informative, and consistent. Educators should be deliberate about 12 homework characteristics. These features individually and collectively can enhance the effectiveness and perceptions of homework.

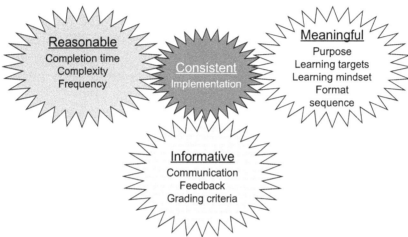

Figure I.1 Deliberate Homework Model

The first three characteristics—(1) completion time, (2) complexity, and (3) frequency—are the foundation of deliberate homework and relate directly to being reasonable. The next five characteristics collectively explain why meaningful homework includes deliberate (4) purpose, (5) learning targets, (6) learning mindset, (7) format, and (8) sequence. The next three characteristics—(9) communication, (10) feedback, and (11) grading criteria—collectively define how to make homework informative. Finally, characteristic (12), deliberate implementation, connects all of the characteristics and explains recommendations for reviewing and creating consistent homework belief statements and practices. Your answer to the question below should be guided by the 12 characteristics of deliberate homework. This question will be revisited in the final chapter of this book.

Table I.1 Guiding Primary Question Regarding Deliberate Homework

Guiding Primary Question	Your Response
What criteria guide decisions for assigning every homework assignment?	

The following concise summary of recommendations aligns with the sequence of these 12 characteristics and provides a general preview for this book. Deliberate homework allows for multiple days to be completed, is differentiated, assigned only once or twice a week, is purposeful, and is aligned to learning targets. Deliberate homework empowers meaningful practice, creativity, connections, and/or reflection; it is meaningful and effective and includes understandable two-way communication. It is evaluated via fair and understandable grading criteria; includes concise and purposeful feedback that empowers improvement; aligns with students' learning mindsets that includes being responsible, resilient, reflective, resourceful, and receptive to feedback; and the homework is consistently and purposefully implemented.

General recommendations for each of these 12 characteristics are discussed in subsequent chapters. The brief informative chapters lay contextualizing foundations for deliberate and reflective discussions that will shape homework practices for students in elementary, middle, and high schools. Each characteristic is defined via exploration about the significance regarding the what, why, and how to be deliberate. Each chapter concludes with ten deliberate continuous learning questions, images, presentation slides, or challenges that guide independent or collaborative professional learning about homework practices to empower reflective learning and unlearning with a growth mindset.

SECTION

I

Reasonable Homework

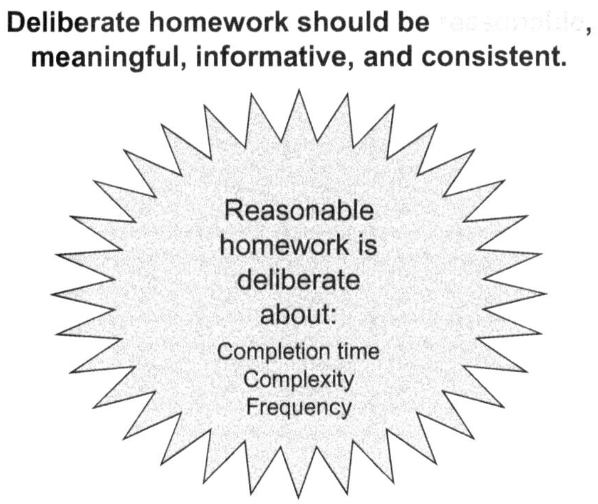
Deliberate homework should be reasonable,
meaningful, informative, and consistent.
Reasonable
homework is
deliberate
about:
Completion time
Complexity
Frequency

Figure S.1 Reasonable homework

1

Completion Time

Reasonable homework is an aspect of deliberate homework defined by completion time, complexity, and frequency, which are learning equity challenges that are the foundation of deliberate homework and should guide the explanation of and justification for reasonable homework.

Completion time refers to the amount of time needed to complete homework and could include the number of days students have to finish the assignment. Teachers should be cognizant of the total amount of homework completion time assigned across all classes in which the student is currently enrolled. Communication with other teachers is vital for planning the amount of homework to assign in addition to making sure that the completion time for homework for all classes is reasonable. Completion time is discussed in this chapter; complexity will be explored in Chapter 2; and frequency will be a focus for Chapter 3. Before reading this chapter, please take a few minutes to respond to the self-assessment statements below.

Table 1.1 Self-Assessment of Current Homework Practices

	Never	Rarely	Sometimes	Often	Always
I understand the amount of time my low ability students spend on most homework assignments.					
I know how much time my students spend on homework for me and other teachers each week.					
I allow multiple days to complete homework assignments.					
I understand how all of my students spend their time when not in school.					
I gather feedback about homework challenges my students experience and provide support.					
I assign homework that reflects the different growth rates of my students.					

What

Homework completion time can range on a continuum that includes unrealistic or sporadic expectations, recommended maximum minutes for nightly homework, or allowing multiple nights for students to complete an assignment. Naturally, homework completion time varies by student and by the complexity of the assignment. Some students will complete the activity more quickly than classmates, while others will complete the activity more slowly or not at all. Variables to consider include differences amongst the cognitive abilities of students, their knowledge of the topic, individual organizational and problem-solving skills, adult support, and family or student activities such as sports or community commitments that occupy time outside of the school day. Figure 1.1 provides a visual of what some teachers think homework looks like, while Figures 1.2 and 1.3 provide a glimpse of what homework looks like in my house.

Teachers must understand the potential challenges their students encounter as well as supports that could enhance short and long-term success. Educators

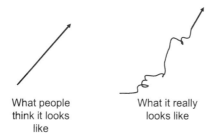

Homework

What people think it looks like

What it really looks like

Figure 1.1 Some Teachers Think Homework Looks like …

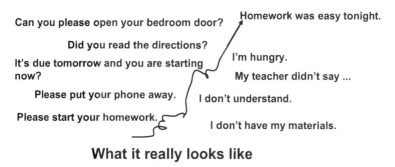

Homework

Can you please open your bedroom door?

Homework was easy tonight.

Did you read the directions?

It's due tomorrow and you are starting now?

I'm hungry.

My teacher didn't say …

Please put your phone away.

I don't understand.

Please start your homework.

I don't have my materials.

What it really looks like

Figure 1.2 Homework in Some Homes

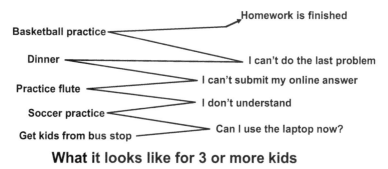

Homework

Homework is finished

Basketball practice

Dinner

I can't do the last problem

I can't submit my online answer

Practice flute

I don't understand

Soccer practice

Get kids from bus stop

Can I use the laptop now?

What it looks like for 3 or more kids

Figure 1.3 Homework in My Home

can differentiate homework completion time by granting multiple days for students to complete homework assignments thus allowing students to plan around other activities and complete the work when they have time. Teachers can also assign homework that encompasses targeted and concise skill practice.

Challenges teachers may encounter when allowing more than one day to complete homework include the need for proper planning and progress monitoring to ensure sequential learning and that students understand foundation skills before introducing or practicing more complex skills or ideas. However, this planning challenge should be an expected complexity of the process rather than a reason not to provide multiple days to complete homework.

Why

Homework completion time is a learning equity problem when some students do not have the resources or ability to independently complete homework assignments. Thoughtless planning about homework completion time is an equity problem that can result in excessive or unreasonable amounts of time spent on homework. Sometimes the homework is excessive for all students, and sometimes the amount of time spent on homework is only unreasonable for students struggling with the assignment or students who do not have access to help with understanding directions or completing tasks. The home environment of every student must be considered by teachers so that task differentiation can make homework reasonable. A focus on completion time is the most impactful feature that could independently resolve homework concerns by helping students rather than enhancing their stress and by appeasing parents rather than frustrating them. Teachers must first understand how many minutes it takes for every student to complete homework. Focusing on how many minutes it takes for a high ability student to complete their homework while being oblivious to how long it takes a struggling student (who already probably struggled in the classroom) is short-sighted and neglectful.

The excessive time spent working on homework can directly or indirectly limit participation in extracurricular activities and planned family activities and can increase stress at home for students and/or parents. Homework completion time can be more reasonable when teachers are conscious of the number of homework problems or questions they assign. Further, educators can understand the potential negative impact homework has when students are involved in extracurricular activities, have additional family or employment responsibilities, or lack support or materials at home. Allowing multiple days to complete homework assignments empowers students to demonstrate ownership of the completion of the task. This student choice can decrease the stress of having to stay up late to finish homework when students are empowered to decide to complete homework on the days they do not have additional responsibilities. Changes regarding homework completion time must also consider the variables of homework complexity and frequency since these characteristics can be leveraged to make changes in the impact of, the beliefs about, and the effectiveness of, homework.

How

Rather than being excessive or burdensome, homework completion time for deliberate homework is succinct and takes into account other school activities and responsibilities. The quality of the homework is emphasized rather than the quantity. Teachers should analyze a potential homework assignment and select a few questions or problems that align with current student needs. Selecting a limited amount of questions to answer enables teachers to exclude questions or problems that do not align with current student needs, allows for task differentiation, and helps limit the amount of time spent on homework altogether. Instead of assigning homework while only thinking about what happens in one's own classroom, deliberately assigned homework is collaboratively planned with other teachers so students have a reasonable amount of homework. An example is assigning one or two quality homework questions or practice problems at the correct complexity, rather than multiple mediocre, low level, less meaningful, or unnecessary questions or problems and allowing multiple days to complete.

Flexibility of work completion results when an educator deliberately plans homework and provides multiple days for its execution. Deliberately planned homework does not prevent students from participating in extracurricular activities, spending quality time with family members, or getting adequate sleep. Teachers encourage ownership and time management development as well as being active outside of school by allowing multiple days for homework assignments to be completed. Students with multiple nightly obligations on some nights (or every night) can budget their time to complete homework on the night they have the most unstructured time. This change can decrease stress and increase time management and ownership. Options include, for instance, assigning homework on Monday that is due Wednesday or always having a specific type of homework assignment due on Fridays. This predictability allows for a better estimation of completion time.

Related topics for additional research about deliberate homework completion time include empathy and relationships. Teachers can enhance their understanding of how long it takes students to complete homework by first connecting with students and truly examining their diverse needs, backgrounds, and levels of confidence with regard to homework. With thoughtful exploration, teachers can learn more about their students as well as identify those in need of additional support, encouragement, and differentiation to foster homework completion. Understanding your student population will guide how, when, what, and why you teach. Teaching routines and self-help strategies before assigning homework can also decrease completion time. These topics will be further discussed in subsequent chapters.

Table 1.2 Guiding Primary Questions Regarding Homework Completion Time

Guiding Primary Questions	Your Response
How many minutes will it take to complete this homework assignment for the student who understands directions and concepts and has all of the resources? How many minutes will it take for a student who does not understand the concepts and may be missing some of the resources?	
How much time do your students spend on homework for you versus other teachers each day? Each week?	
How many accurate answers does a student need to demonstrate proficiency?	
How can you empower ownership so students self-assess and recognize understanding and do not need additional independent practice?	

Answers to these four questions can guide a teacher's reflection about changes or differentiation that would limit the assignment of more homework practice than is needed. Teachers must understand how students spend their time when not in school, gather feedback about existing homework challenges, and analyze potential challenges so their students are not overburdened by the amount of time spent on homework. The following implementation planner and reflection questions can guide discussions and potential homework improvements with regard to completion time.

Table 1.3 Chapter Implementation Planner for Homework Completion Time

Topics I will ...	Responses
Investigate	
Discuss	
Reflect on	
Change	

D.E.L.I.B.E.R.A.T.E. Continuous Improvement Questions for Homework Completion Time

The following D.E.L.I.B.E.R.A.T. E. questions can guide reflection, discussion, and professional learning by asking you to Differentiate, Explain, Learn, Implement, Bolster, Empower, Reflect, Ask, Terminate, and Entrust.

- *Differentiate* prioritized expectations for an absent student: students who are absent for multiple days need scaffolded guidance to help them understand learning they missed. How will you use this process to prioritize the work the student missed while absent?

Prioritized Homework for Absent Student

Student Name: ____________________

Teacher Name: ____________________

Date: ____________________

Welcome back! Please complete the prioritized homework in the order listed on the chart below. Homework modifications are not always made for absent students. However, new learning is building on the work you missed, so noted below is learning practice with a few modified expectations regarding the amount of work and time you have to complete the work.

Please complete the following circled homework first: New Homework Absence Homework

Subject	Resource/Materials	Assignment Explanation (Pages and problem #s)	Modified Expectation	Modified Due Date

Optional practice IF additional practice is still needed: ____________________

Classmates who can support or help you if you have clarifying questions: ____________________

Figure 1.4 Prioritized Homework for Absent Student

- *Explain* what you will do to better understand how much time each of your students is spending on homework and how the homework is informing teaching and learning.

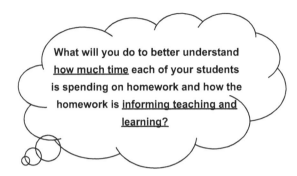

Figure 1.5 How Much Time?

Explain the outcomes of your homework time analysis. How will you prevent your homework from having a negative influence on participation in family activities or sports? A supporting activity is to ask students to write down the amount of time spent discussing and working on homework so you can make changes and provide support as needed. A second step is to ask students to create a goal for themselves and recommend changes to make homework more reasonable, meaningful, and infrequent. Explain the outcomes of your homework time analysis.

HOMEWORK Time

Understanding the amount of time parents discuss (or argue about) homework while encouraging their child to begin their homework can guide meaningful changes that reduce stress, enhance efficiency and foster independence. For one week, ask students and parents to document the amount of time they discuss homework each day as well as the amount of time the child spends on homework. Based on the results, write a goal for you and recommendations for me to consider:

Goal:_____

		5	10	15	20	25	30	35	40	40+
Sunday	Discussing									
	Working									
Saturday	Discussing									
	Working									
Friday	Discussing									
	Working									
Thursday	Discussing									
	Working									
Wednesday	Discussing									
	Working									
Tuesday	Discussing									
	Working									
Monday	Discussing									
	Working									

Figure 1.6 Time Analysis

◆ *Learn* how you can make homework assignments more concise and efficient. How can you demonstrate flexibility and allow multiple days for homework completion?

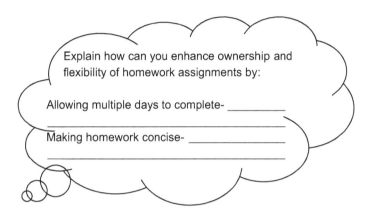

Explain how can you enhance ownership and flexibility of homework assignments by:

Allowing multiple days to complete- _____
_____
Making homework concise- _____
_____

Figure 1.7 Ownership and Flexibility

◆ *Implement*: Explain how you are communicating and collaborating with fellow teachers so nightly homework is not excessively burdensome.

How are you communicating and collaborating with fellow teachers so nightly homework is not excessively burdensome **for students and their families?**

Figure 1.8 Not Excessively Burdensome

◆ *Bolster*: Which project will this long-term project planner be used to bolster guidance and support for students?

	Long-Term Project Planner				
Name: _____		Assignment: _____		Due Date: _____	
Goal	What	Planning Notes or Reminders	Reflection About Progress or Potential Improvements	Date Started	Date Completed
1	Complete this planning guide based on success criteria and expectations.				
2	Identify necessary materials and resources.				
3	Create a general outline or plan on the back of this planning guide.				
4	Describe First Step: _____ _____				
5	Describe Next Steps: _____ _____				
6	Seek feedback from classmate, teacher, or parent and reflect on feedback and recommendations.				
7	Describe Final Steps: _____ _____				
8	Review success criteria gain, verify all expectations are met, and check for accuracy and neatness.				

Figure 1.9 Long-Term Project Planner

◆ *Empower* students to self-assess and communicate whether or not they are capable of practicing a skill, process, standard, or strategy independently. How can your current homework practices align with this statement?

If homework is additional practice of a skill, process, standard or strategy, ensure students have had meaningful guided and independent practice at school so frequency and amount of homework are both reasonable.

Figure 1.10 Meaningful Guided and Independent Practice

Examine Figures 1.11 and 1.12 and reflect upon how you can empower your students by limiting weekly minutes of homework and assigning self-directed homework.

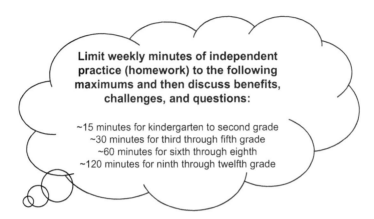

Figure 1.11 Limit Weekly Minutes of Independent Practice

Self-directed five-minute homework

Select two skills or topics to practice two nights for five minutes each night.

1. Identify areas of focus: _____

2. Explain how you will practice: _____
_____

At the end of the week, reflect about the impact of this flexible self-directed practice.

3. Reflect about your improvement: _____
_____
_____
_____

Figure 1.12 Self-Directed Five-Minute Homework

◆ *Reflect* on a recent homework assignment and explain the thoughts and perspectives that each of these students and parents might possess.

Homework reflection

Reflect about a recent homework assignment and explain the different thoughts and perspectives that each of these students and parents might have:

Transient or low income student: _____

Below average student: _____

Above average student: _____

Student-athlete: _____

_____

Parent of 5 children: _____

Parent who works at night: _____

Parent who can't help with homework: _____

_____

Potential changes I will make based on my reflection about different student and parent perspectives and needs:_____

Figure 1.13 Homework Reflection

◆ *Ask* students and parents: About how many minutes a week do your students attend to homework? Reflect on the responses and explain ways you could decrease this amount. The homework assignment completion time critique questions can guide your reflection.

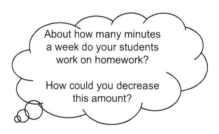

About how many minutes a week do your students work on homework?

How could you decrease this amount?

Figure 1.14 How Could You Decrease Homework?

What routines and self-help strategies can you teach students before assigning homework?

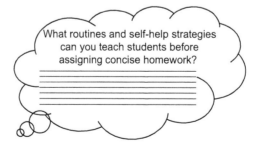

What routines and self-help strategies can you teach students before assigning concise homework?

Figure 1.15 Routines and Strategies

Homework assignment completion time
Critique questions

1. Which questions can you differentiate?
2. Which complex problem should be discussed in class before being worked on at home?
3. What strategies can students use when they are unsuccessful while working independently at home?

Figure 1.16 Homework Assignment Completion Time Critique Questions

◆ *Terminate*: Educators recognize the benefits of inspiring a love for reading. Don't assign excessive daily homework that interferes with having time to read. How can your current homework practices terminate this negative impact?

Educators recognize the benefits of inspiring a love for reading.

Don't assign excessive daily homework that interferes with having time to read before getting a good night sleep.

Figure 1.17 Don't Assign Excessive Homework that Interferes with Reading and Sleep

◆ *Entrust* students to practice math for 15 minutes rather than mandating the number of problems. Then ask students to discuss how effective their practice was with a partner and evaluate the difficulty level of the math problems they solved.

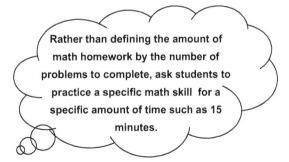

Rather than defining the amount of math homework by the number of problems to complete, ask students to practice a specific math skill for a specific amount of time such as 15 minutes.

Figure 1.18 Specific Amount of Time

2

Complexity

Homework complexity refers to the difficulty level of homework questions and assignments and an awareness of how the difficulty aligns with individual needs, skills, and mindsets. Homework complexity is a learning equity problem that can be positively or negatively impacted by students' experiences, understanding, and access to support, resources, or assistance. Teachers must understand the potential challenges their students encounter as well as supports that could enhance short and long-term success. Homework complexity directly impacts previously discussed homework completion time; thus, teachers should recognize the impact of potential complexity changes that could be made for students who spend excessive amounts of time attending to homework. Before reading this chapter, please take a few minutes to respond to the self-assessment statements below.

Table 2.1 Self-Assessment of Current Homework Practices

	Never	Rarely	Sometimes	Often	Always
My homework questions align with grade level expectations, but I align difficulty or support with individual student needs.					
I informally assess student understanding and comfort level during guided practice before assigning independent practice or homework.					
My homework is differentiated by amount, content, process, product, ability, readiness, or learning style.					
My homework empowers student ownership by enhancing understanding of their capabilities and progress.					
I assign homework that incorporates basic and complex questions.					

What

Similar to purpose, learning target, and sequence, homework complexity should align with recent performance. Thus, if a student demonstrates their understanding of the basic concept or skill, complexity of their independent practice and homework should be more challenging. Similarly, if a student does not demonstrate an understanding of the basic concept or skill (yet), the complexity of their independent practice and homework should be reduced.

Teachers should understand what each student knows and is able to do. Teachers should also recognize that the complexity of questions when guided by teacher support should look different than the complexity during independent practice such as homework. Teachers mindful of homework complexity ask questions that align with grade-level expectations, though they increase the difficulty or supports to align with an individual student's needs. Educators mindful of homework complexity and the progression of skill scaffold supports during initial learning activities before empowering independence as learners demonstrate understanding. When mindful of homework complexity, teachers informally assess students' understanding and comfort levels during guided practice before assigning independent practice or homework. Additional modifications such as leveraging technology to target specific complexity levels can differentiate for each student's needs.

Differentiated teaching and learning can limit the need for differentiated homework because the complexity already aligns with student needs. Homework that is differentiated for every student may be unrealistic. However, differentiated types of homework for two to four groups can be more effective. Teachers who efficiently engage students with fair but high homework expectations at their ability level will empower problem solving, reflection, and students making connections. Deliberate homework complexity is at the correct difficulty level for every student and is differentiated by the amount, content, process, product, ability, readiness, or learning style. Teachers who are cognizant of deliberate homework complexity ask different levels of questions, based on students' readiness, to encourage them to enhance their understanding by applying, analyzing, evaluating, or creating.

Educators who are not mindful of homework complexity may inequitably assign the same homework to all students regardless of their readiness, which results in struggling learners spending more time on homework than do proficient learners. Unmindful homework complexity can look like the stereotype busywork where higher ability students finish homework quickly that is too difficult for lower ability students to finish independently or in a reasonable amount of time.

Why

Homework complexity should be reasonable and should align with student abilities. Homework complexity that is too easy can be viewed as a waste of time while homework that is too difficult can result in the student thinking "Why bother?" Additional possible outcomes for homework that is too difficult include students depending on assistance from classmates or parents, or students writing down copied answers. Assigning reasonable and meaningful homework with a complexity that aligns with students' needs and abilities is critical yet difficult. This process happens when students are taught how to self-assess their understanding, evaluate their progress, and establish goals compared to expectations, grade-level skills, or standards. The correct homework complexity empowers students to embrace opportunities for productive challenges that include grappling with and making sense of information during a process of continuous growth and improvement.

How

The complexity curve shown in Figure 2.1 illustrates that an independent productive struggle is a sweet spot for homework complexity that is between being too easy or too difficult. Support in the classroom includes guided practice, scaffolded supports, modeling and practicing strategies, checking for understanding, starting homework in class, and making time to discuss student questions about the homework. Out of class homework supports include providing or recommending helpful resources that students and/or parents can refer to, as needed. Ideal outcomes when complexity aligns with students' abilities include goal setting, independent problem solving, application, continuous improvement with a growth mindset, and self-assessment of progress.

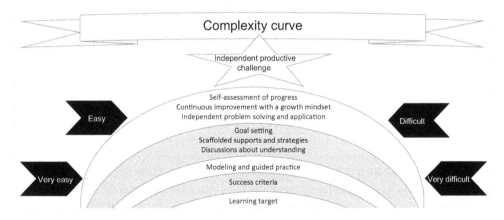

Figure 2.1 Complexity Curve

Figure 2.2 illustrates an example of deliberate homework complexity that first focuses on guided and independent practice in class so teachers can check for understanding and provide feedback. Educators then assign differentiated homework based on need by including four different options such as additional practice, more complex practice, application of knowledge, or student-created choice or reflection. Additional complexity modifications

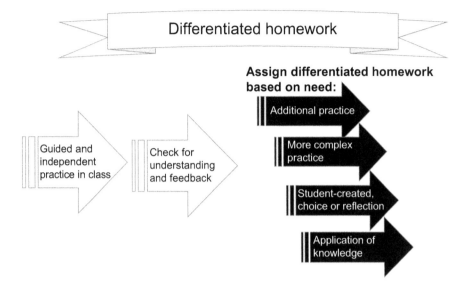

Figure 2.2 Differentiated Homework

include modifying the process or amount of time that students must devote to homework.

Table 2.2 Guiding Primary Questions Regarding Homework Complexity

Guiding Primary Question	Your Response
How can inequity of homework for certain students empower change related to how you provide independent practice for all students?	
How will you empower students to own their learning and enhance their understanding of their own capabilities and progress?	

The following implementation planner and reflection questions can guide discussions and potential homework improvements for complexity.

Table 2.3 Chapter Implementation Planner for Homework Complexity

Topics I will ...	Responses
Investigate	
Discuss	
Reflect on	
Change	

D.E.L.I.B.E.R.A.T.E. Continuous Improvement Questions for Homework Complexity

The following D.E.L.I.B.E.R.A.T.E. questions can guide reflection, discussion, and professional learning by asking you to Differentiate, Explain, Learn, Implement, Bolster, Empower, Reflect, Ask, Terminate, and Entrust.

◆ *Differentiate*: How is your homework differentiated, or what supports are in place for the student who (1) understands the concept and does not need additional practice or who (2) does not understand and will not be able to finish independently?

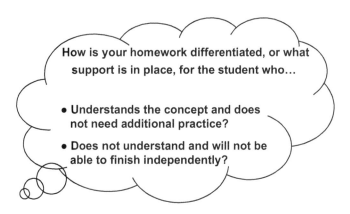

Figure 2.3 How Is Your Homework Differentiated?

◆ *Explain*: Complexity can be guided by deliberate questions. What reflection question(s) will you ask your students to empower them to explain their thinking about how they created meaning by forming a big idea from a unit or explaining how their thinking evolved.

Explain your thinking

Name: _____ Date: _____ Chapter/Unit: _____

Explain how you created meaning about a big idea or explain how your thinking evolved while reading and discussing the previous chapter or unit.

_____
_____
_____
_____
_____
_____
_____
_____
_____

Figure 2.4 Explain Your Thinking

◆ *Learn*: What differentiated modifications or supportive scaffolds can make deliberate homework more equitable and reasonable for every student in your class, school, or school district?

What differentiated modifications or supportive scaffolds can make deliberate homework more equitable and reasonable for every student in your class, school, or school district?

Figure 2.5 Equitable and Reasonable Homework

◆ *Implement* differentiated concise homework by asking questions that vary in levels of complexity. Formally or informally document individual student progress on the different levels of questions and use gathered data to guide the complexity of homework by isolating practice with one to four questions given at levels of difficulty that each student can complete independently.

Differentiated concise homework

- Ask questions that vary in levels of complexity.
- Formally or informally document individual student progress on the different levels of questions.
- Use gathered data to guide complexity of homework by isolating practice with 1–4 questions at levels of difficulty that each student can complete independently.

Figure 2.6 Differentiated Concise Homework

◆ *Bolster*: Enhancing rigor does not equal more homework. How will you bolster critical thinking rather than assigning more homework?

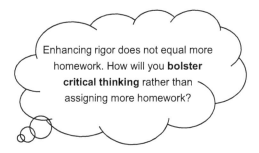

Enhancing rigor does not equal more homework. How will you **bolster critical thinking** rather than assigning more homework?

Figure 2.7 Bolster Critical Thinking

◆ *Empower* ownership, choice and self-regulation: What choices will you give students to enhance alignment between homework complexity and all students' abilities?

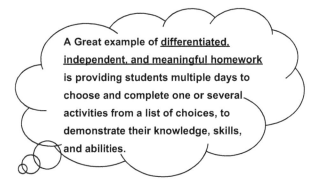

A Great example of <u>differentiated, independent, and meaningful homework</u> is providing students multiple days to choose and complete one or several activities from a list of choices, to demonstrate their knowledge, skills, and abilities.

Figure 2.8 Differentiated, Independent, and Meaningful Homework

◆ *Reflect*: How can "Performance-Based Math Homework" and "Student-Created Personalized Homework" guide future homework options in your classroom, school, or school district? How can one differentiate more for content, process, product, or ability?

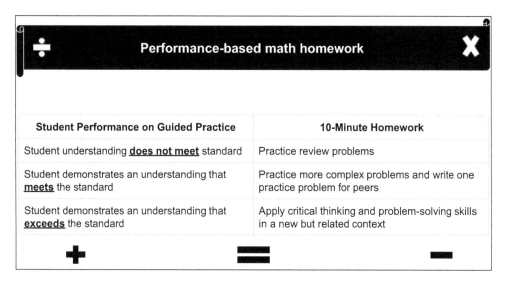

Performance-based math homework

Student Performance on Guided Practice	10-Minute Homework
Student understanding **does not meet** standard	Practice review problems
Student demonstrates an understanding that **meets** the standard	Practice more complex problems and write one practice problem for peers
Student demonstrates an understanding that **exceeds** the standard	Apply critical thinking and problem-solving skills in a new but related context

Figure 2.9 Performance-Based Math Homework

Student-created personalized homework

Name: _____ Date: _____ Subject: _____

1. Identified need:
A. The skill, standard or topic I want to enhance proficiency, speed, accuracy or fluency for: _____
_____

B. I will practice this identified target by: _____
_____

2. Self-assessment and reflection after completion of personalized homework:
A. My self-assessment of the difficulty level (circle one):   Easy   Challenging   Difficult
B. My self-assessment of my understanding (circle one):   Below   Approaching   Meets   Extends

C. Recommended next steps to continue to practice this identified skill or a related skill: _____
_____
_____
_____

*Attach this reflection to your completed, student-created personalized homework

Figure 2.10 Student-Created Personalized Homework

◆ *Ask*: What can you ask to better comprehend student understanding and confidence with regard to homework assignments?

If homework is additional practice of a skill, process, standard, or strategy, ensure students have had meaningful, guided, and independent practice at school so frequency and amount of homework are both reasonable.

Figure 2.11 Ensure Meaningful Guided and Independent Practice

◆ *Terminate*: Which homework assignments will you terminate?

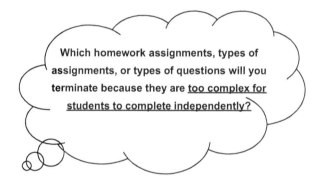

Which homework assignments, types of assignments, or types of questions will you terminate because they are <u>too complex for students to complete independently?</u>

Figure 2.12 Terminate Complex Homework

◆ *Entrust*: How can you enhance student choice regarding homework complexity?

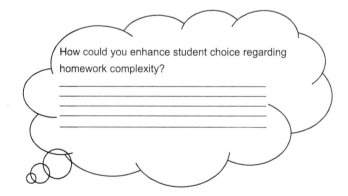

How could you enhance student choice regarding homework complexity?

Figure 2.13 Enhance Student Complexity with Choice

3

Frequency

Homework frequency is the number of days each week that homework is assigned. Deliberate homework frequency should also consider the impact of completion time and complexity because infrequent homework will still be a problem if it is too complex and takes students excessive time to complete. Before reading this chapter, please take a few minutes to answer the self-assessment questions below.

Table 3.1 Self-Assessment of Current Homework Practices

	Never	Rarely	Sometimes	Often	Always
I assign daily homework.					
I assign three or more days of homework a week.					
I assign homework on the weekend.					
I assign homework on holiday breaks.					

What

Your purpose for homework should guide decisions about homework frequency and complexity. Deliberate frequency of homework recognizes the differences and impacts homework assignments may have on students and families. Deliberate homework is assigned occasionally rather than daily and is not assigned when school is closed for a holiday or extended break. Deliberate planning recognizes that holidays and vacations are for memories, not homework. Deliberate frequency of homework recognizes that students have families and events outside of school.

Please remember that rigor does not equal daily homework. Working with high-achieving students or teaching advanced classes does not mean more homework must be assigned. Thoughtless frequency of homework assigns it daily regardless of learning needs. Assigning daily homework may unfortunately focus more on assigning any type of homework rather than concise targeted practice only when it is needed. A related topic for additional research about deliberate homework frequency is motivation.

Why

Benefits of occasional and deliberate homework include providing reasonable practice to enhance accuracy, understanding, growth, and learning. School districts must understand needs, demands, and preferences of community stakeholders as they define the purpose for the homework. Parents have different school and homework experiences and have different homework expectations for their child that range from daily to never. Some stakeholders may embrace daily homework, while other stakeholders may prefer zero homework. Some parents may want daily rigorous homework to prepare their children to become successful in the future and to keep them productively busy rather than playing video games, while other parents are too busy to help with homework because of their job or a busy home life that includes preparing dinner and driving children to sports and activities. Potential negative impacts when teachers are not deliberate about frequency include too much or too frequent homework that stresses students out and affects time spent with family and on other activities. Challenges teachers may encounter include parent expectations and comparisons with other teachers and grade levels.

How

Teachers should effectively plan learning to maximize active participation, cognitive engagement, and differentiation so that meaningful, deliberate, and efficient homework is only needed occasionally. Teachers can also differentiate homework frequency based on student need. One solution is to count the typical number of weekly homework assignments and reduce this number by replacing them with less frequent and more focused and concise homework. Another solution is to create more opportunities for students to work on homework at school. This independent practice time at school with the teacher allows for students to be supported as needed. Another potential solution is to limit homework frequency to no more than once or twice a week.

Sometimes students have multiple assessments on the same day that require a lot of preparation for the next one before the exams. For example, teachers typically want to assess on Friday and start a new unit of study on Monday. However, this mindset can be redefined for some subjects. Friday could be used for reflection, goal setting, or pre-learning. If homework is not occasional enough, a more rigid option is trying the schedule proposed in Figure 3.1 for a month and evaluating the impact. The schedule limits the nights that homework can be assigned and designates one day of the week on which assessments can be administered. Homework could help prepare and check for understanding of the assessment the next day, or the homework could be unrelated to the assessment. This schedule can help students plan in advance and help avoid burdening them with homework in multiple classes. It may be too rigid, but it also may ultimately decrease the frequency and dependency on homework. This frequency solution can decrease the number of nights students have to study at home for Friday assessments in multiple classes while increasing ungraded informal formative assessment activities that affect future instruction. To maximize impact, teachers will still have to be aware of the completion time and complexity of the homework they assign.

	Monday	Tuesday	Wednesday	Thursday	Friday	Weekend
Homework Due Date	Social Studies	Science	Math	Language Arts		
Assessment		Social Studies	Science	Math	Language Arts	

Figure 3.1 Weekly Assessment and Homework Schedule

Table 3.2 Guiding Primary Question Regarding Homework Frequency

Guiding Primary Question	Your Response
What changes will you need to make to help students benefit from a maximum of one night of weekly homework?	
If you think of homework as practice, what practice opportunities can you provide in your classroom rather than assign as homework?	

The following implementation planner and reflection questions can guide discussions and potential homework improvements for frequency.

Table 3.3 Chapter Implementation Planner for Homework Frequency

Topics I will ...	Responses
Investigate	
Discuss	
Reflect on	
Change	

D.E.L.I.B.E.R.A.T.E. Continuous Improvement Questions for Homework Frequency

The following D.E.L.I.B.E.R.A.T.E questions can guide reflection, discussion, and professional learning by asking you to Differentiate, Explain, Learn, Implement, Bolster, Empower, Reflect, Ask, Terminate, and Entrust.

◆ *Differentiate*: How can you differentiate homework frequency for different students during different times of the year?

Differentiate homework frequency

Step 1. How can you differentiate homework frequency for different students during different times of the year?

_____
_____
_____
_____
_____
_____
_____
_____

Step 2. Discuss response with colleagues.

Figure 3.2 Differentiate Homework Frequency

◆ *Explain* your rationale for the number of days students should have homework to a colleague and listen to his or her response. Discuss with a colleague how your answer changes for two-day weekends, three-day weekends, or extended breaks. What intentional modifications can be made to decrease the number of days that homework is assigned?

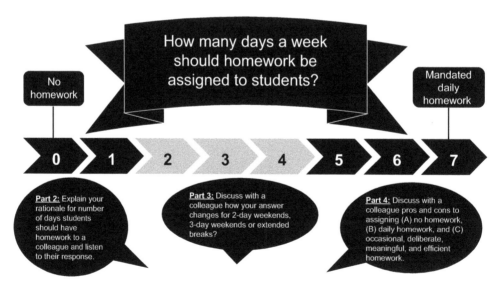

Figure 3.3 How Many Days a Week Should Homework Be Assigned?

◆ *Learn*: What questions will you ask your students and parents about the type and amount of homework you assign?

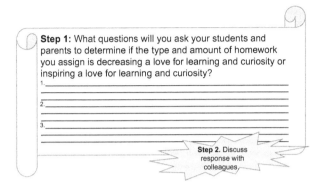

Step 1: What questions will you ask your students and parents to determine if the type and amount of homework you assign is decreasing a love for learning and curiosity or inspiring a love for learning and curiosity?

1._____
2._____
3._____

Step 2. Discuss response with colleagues.

Figure 3.4 Ask to Determine the Impact on Love for Learning

◆ *Implement*: How can you modify learning in your classroom to incorporate more time for independent practice, student discussion, and feedback to ultimately decrease the amount and frequency of homework?

How can you modify learning in your classroom to incorporate more time for independent practice, student discussion, and feedback to ultimately decrease the amount and frequency of homework?

Figure 3.5 How Can You Modify Learning?

◆ *Bolster* home opportunities by not assigning homework some weeks.

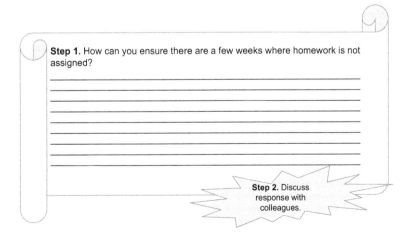

Step 1. How can you ensure there are a few weeks where homework is not assigned?

Step 2. Discuss response with colleagues.

Figure 3.6 A Few Weeks Where Homework Is Not Assigned

◆ *Empower* collaboration: How will you collaboratively discuss weekly homework expectations with your colleagues so students are not overwhelmed by homework assigned from multiple teachers on the same nights?

Step 1: How will you collaboratively discuss weekly homework expectations with your colleagues so students are not overwhelmed with homework assigned from multiple teachers on the same nights?

Step 2. Discuss response with colleagues.

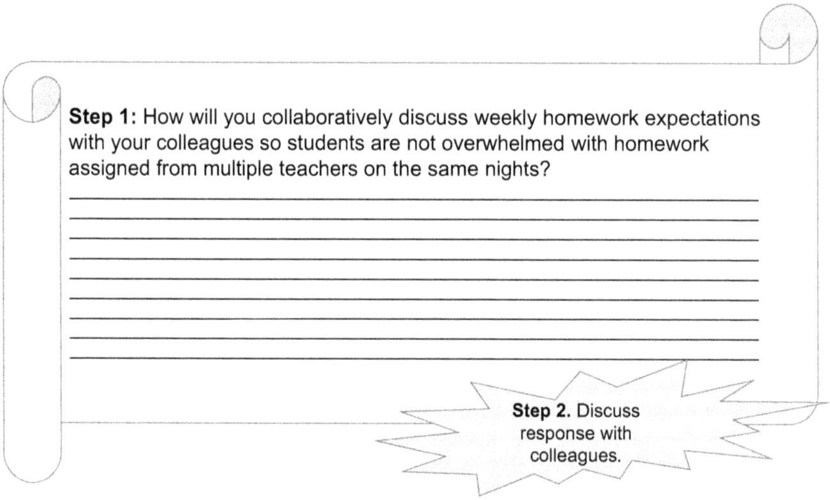

Figure 3.7 Collaboratively Discuss

◆ *Reflect*: What changes need to be made so homework is only assigned one night a week?

Step 1: What changes need to be made so homework is only assigned one night a week?

Step 2. Discuss response with colleagues.

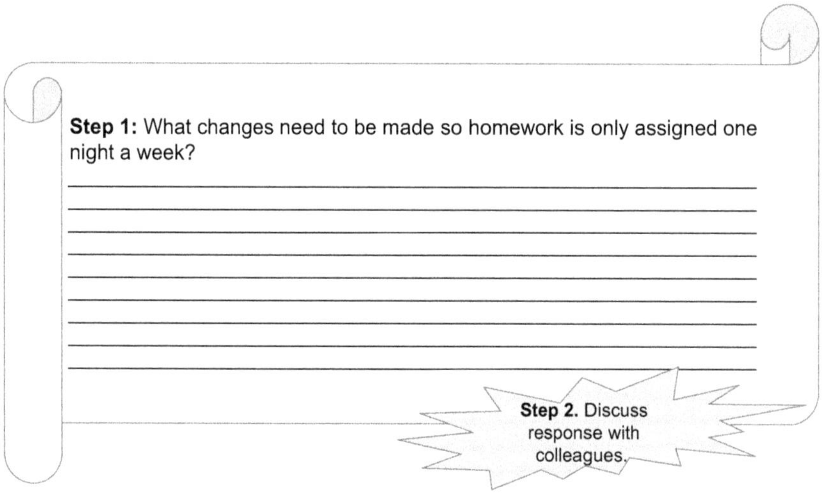

Figure 3.8 One Night a Week

- *Ask*: What three questions can you ask students or parents to better understand their comfort level regarding the frequency of assigned homework?

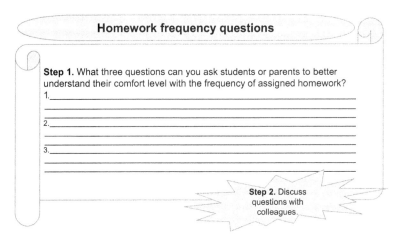

Figure 3.9 Homework Frequency Questions

- *Terminate*: What changes will you make so homework is not assigned on weekends and holidays?

Holidays and vacations are for memories not homework!

Figure 3.10 Holidays and Vacations Are for Memories

- *Entrust*: How can you enhance student choice regarding the homework format?

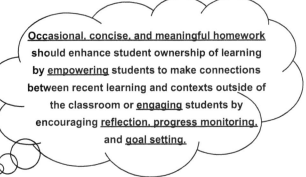

Figure 3.11 Student Choice Regarding Homework Format

Information from this and the previous two chapters can collectively define whether or not your homework assignments are reasonable. Table 3.4 can be used to evaluate how reasonable any homework assignment is based on the characteristics discussed in this book. You can evaluate homework by writing a checkmark under reasonable or unreasonable items listed for each criteria. Modifications for some or all students include differentiating, enhancing, decreasing, or not assigning parts or all of the homework.

Table 3.4 Reasonable Homework Criteria

	Criteria	Reasonable	Unreasonable
Completion time	The approximate amount of time my low ability students will spend on this homework assignment is …		
	The approximate amount of time my students will spend on homework for me and other teachers this week is …		
	This homework assignment reflects the different growth rates of my students that are …		
	The opportunities for students to self-assess or recognize when they understand and do not need additional independent practice are …		
Complexity	The homework questions align with grade-level expectations, and enhanced difficulty or support aligns with individual student needs in a way that is …		
	I informally assessed student understanding and comfort level during guided practice before assigning independent practice or homework in a way that was …		
	This homework empowers students' ownership by enhancing understanding of their capabilities and progress in a way that is …		
	The potential inequity of homework for certain students inspires change in a way that is …		

(Continued)

Table 3.4 (Continued)

	Criteria	Reasonable	Unreasonable
Frequency	This homework assignment is the first or second assigned this week in a way that was …		
	Practice opportunities other than homework were provided in the classroom rather than just as homework in a way that was …		

SECTION

II

Meaningful Homework

Deliberate homework should be reasonable, **meaningful**, informative, and consistent.

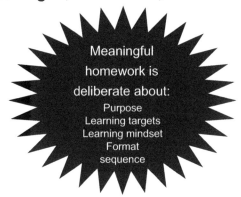

Meaningful
homework is
deliberate about:
Purpose
Learning targets
Learning mindset
Format
sequence

Figure S.2 Meaningful homework is deliberate about

4

Purpose

Meaningful homework is an aspect of deliberate homework defined by purpose, learning targets, learning mindset, format, and sequence. This chapter will focus on purpose; however, a collective focus on purpose, learning targets, learning mindset, format, and sequence will guide our efforts to create and assign homework that is more meaningful for different students at different times in the learning process. Homework purpose could guide homework discussions as did the first chapter in this book; however, purpose is discussed here so that it can build on reflections regarding completion time, complexity, and frequency.

Homework should be purposeful. Focusing on meaningful and targeted activities is more important than the setting where students practice. Hence focusing on these topics can guide homework decisions as well as teaching and learning activities.

Teachers should know and be able to communicate what the learning purpose is for every homework assignment. A simplified focus on purpose results in categorizing most homework as independent practice aligned with recent learning, studying for an assessment, or practicing skills such as vocabulary, spelling, or math computation. Before reading this chapter, please take a few minutes to answer the self-assessment questions below.

Table 4.1 Self-Assessment of Current Homework Practices

	Never	Rarely	Sometimes	Often	Always
I can explain benefits for assigning every homework assignment.					
I make homework more meaningful by thinking of possible intended and unintended messages that each assignment communicates to students and parents.					
Before assigning homework I know and communicate what the learning purpose is for the assignment.					
My homework purposes of practice, differentiation, communication, exploration, and innovation guide my homework decisions.					

What

Teachers should clearly communicate their homework purpose and refer back to it to make homework more meaningful. Deliberate homework purpose should consider individual and shared beliefs regarding: the school district's vision statement; the purpose for the teachers; real-life connections with family, community, and extracurricular activities; the purpose for school/learning; stakeholder expectations; the general purpose for homework; and the purpose for individual homework assignments. Answers to the following seven prompts should collectively guide homework purpose, your homework practices, and discussions regarding each of your homework assignments. Please review Figure 4.1 and then answer the questions in Table 4.2.

Teachers should establish a purpose first to guide planning for meaningful homework. Potential answers to the prompts above could include thoughts such as: the purpose for school is to empower reflective, empathetic and

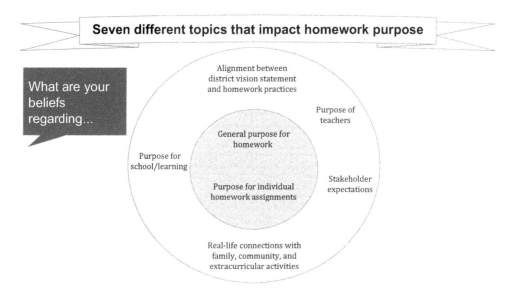

Figure 4.1 Seven Different Topics That Impact Homework Purpose

Table 4.2 Seven Different Topics That Impact Homework Purpose

Beliefs regarding ...	Reflection about Topic
Alignment between district's vision statement and homework practices.	
Purpose of teachers.	
Real-life connections with family, community, and extracurricular activities.	
Purpose for school/learning.	
Stakeholder expectations.	
General purpose for homework.	
Purpose for individual homework assignments.	

curious progress; the purpose for homework is reasonable, meaningful, and informative practice, differentiation, exploration, communication, or innovation. Teachers should clearly communicate their purpose for the homework in general as well as their purpose for individual homework assignments. Teachers should continue to ask why they are assigning homework and gather feedback to critique alignment between their "why" and the assigned homework. Focusing on meaningful, targeted, and purposeful activities is more important than where students practice. Identifying and communicating why you assign homework in general and the purpose for every homework assignment is important.

Why

The purpose helps create reasonable, meaningful, and informative homework. Purposeful homework helps teachers prioritize what learning should occur first and guides planning of other characteristics discussed in this book. Teachers should communicate why homework assignments should be completed. Students should understand why they are completing the homework and how the homework will help improve their learning. Deliberate purposes for homework should be understood and should guide assigned homework. Benefits of a deliberate purpose include a common understanding for students, parents, and teachers.

Potential negative impacts when one is not deliberate about purpose include sporadic focus and inefficient work. Homework should not be a punishment assigned because some students were misbehaving. Misguided purposes for homework can focus mostly on teaching students responsibility or compliance and result in meaningless busywork that provokes excessive stress at home. Examples include using homework as the primary communication to inform parents about what students are learning and/or punishing some students who are misbehaving or not completing assignments. Challenges teachers may encounter include making time to plan and specifying their homework purpose, but the time is well worth it. Related topics for additional research about deliberate homework purpose include vision.

How

Teachers should reflect on the purpose of homework. If the purpose of homework is independent practice, then subsequent decisions can focus on maximizing different types of independent practice inside and outside of the classroom. There are purposes for homework other than independent practice. Different purposes for homework include (1) practice, (2) differentiation, (3) communication, (4) exploration, and (5) innovation. Differentiated meaningful and deliberate independent practice should support learning. Practice focuses on establishing goals and monitoring progress to enhance proficiency, speed, accuracy, or fluency for reading, spelling, vocabulary, math computation, math skills, handwriting, or keyboarding. Practice includes studying, reviewing, reinforcing, or mastering skills and concepts to enhance learning or prepare for an assessment. Practice could also focus on reading. Homework can differentiate responses (amount or complexity), pathways, extension, and rigor. Communication homework can explain, correct, connect, question, teach, discuss, collaborate, justify benefits of new learning, or celebrate growth. Explore how homework empowers students to review, find information and resources, make connections to related topics, reflectively set and monitor goals, choose among options, or do self-directed research. Innovation homework inspires designing, previewing learning content, sharing learning with diverse audiences, extending learning, creating or building. Any of these five purposes for homework could be effective. However, teachers must align their homework format with their homework purpose while being aware of the complexity, completion time, and frequency.

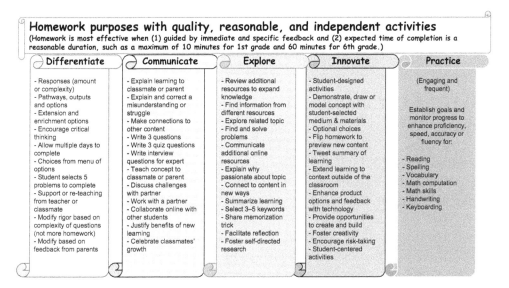

Figure 4.2 Homework Purposes with Quality, Reasonable, and Independent Activities

Table 4.3 Guiding Primary Questions Regarding Homework Purpose

Guiding Primary Question	Your Response
How does your homework enhance or decrease students' passion for curiosity and learning?	
How will you deliberately connect homework to classroom teaching as a means to support and enhance learning?	

The following implementation planner and reflection questions can guide discussions and potential homework improvements for purpose.

Table 4.4 Chapter Implementation Planner for Homework Purpose

Topics I will ...	Responses
Investigate	
Discuss	
Reflect on	
Change	

D.E.L.I.B.E.R.A.T.E. Continuous Improvement Questions for Homework Purpose

The following D.E.L.I.B.E.R.A.T.E. questions can guide reflection, discussion, and professional learning by asking you to Differentiate, Explain, Learn, Implement, Bolster, Empower, Reflect, Ask, Terminate, and Entrust.

◆ *Differentiate*: Use the information below to guide reflection on three ways you can evaluate the purpose of homework at different times during the learning process.

Figure 4.3 Meaningful Homework

◆ *Empower* students to crave ownership, make choices, or self-regulate by changing three homework activities you currently teach to encourage different concise ways students can differentiate, communicate, explore, innovate, or practice.

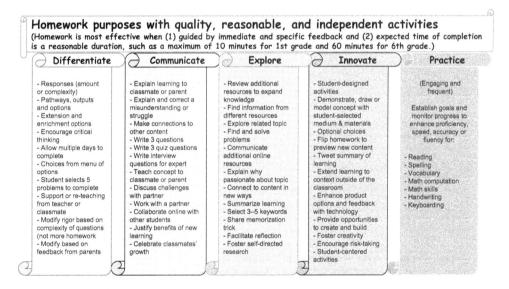

Figure 4.4 Homework Purpose

◆ *Learn*: Learn from students and parents about recommendations to make homework more meaningful, occasional, and deliberate.

Golden rule of
☆ **homework** ☆

**Assign homework that
you would want assigned
to you or your child.** ☆

Figure 4.5 Golden Rule of Homework

◆ *Implement*: Continue to read about and research different ways you can implement homework that is more meaningful, occasional, and deliberate.

Unlearn and change homework

Make homework more reasonable, meaningful, and deliberate

Deliberate homework		Traditional homework
Occasional	**Frequency**	Daily or Never
Concise and efficient	**Amount**	Unreasonable
Differentiated, meaningful, and deliberate independent practice	**Complexity**	Too easy, busy work, or too difficult to complete independently
Provide timely feedback throughout independent practice	**Support**	Provide feedback after learning attempts or not at all
Empower choice regarding process, product, complexity, or amount	**Assignment**	Same assignment for everyone
Multiple days to complete to enhance flexibility	**Due Date**	Due the next day

Figure 4.6 Unlearn and Change Homework

◆ *Bolster*: Bolster three of your homework assignments so they deliberately and efficiently engage students at their ability level and empower problem solving, reflection, or making connections.

**Effective learning deliberately engages students at
their ability level and empowers problem solving,
reflection, or making connections. Similar criteria
should be followed if and when there is a need to
assign independent practice via homework.**

Figure 4.7 Engage Students at Their Ability Level

◆ *Explain*: What next steps will you take to plan engaging classroom learning activities?

Plan engaging classroom learning activities and potential concise and meaningful homework assignments with the consideration that students sit in a classroom for about six hours each school day.

Figure 4.8 Consider Six Hours of Sitting

◆ *Reflect*: Does homework for your students align with your school district's vision or mission statements?

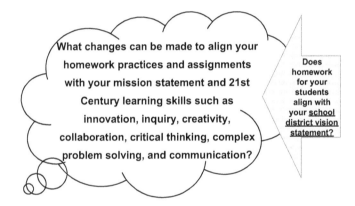

Figure 4.9 Alignment with Vision and Mission

◆ *Ask* students to explain why they are completing each homework assignment with a classmate.

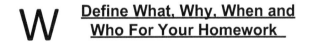

Define What, Why, When and Who For Your Homework

What: Clearly describe directions and expectations.

Why: Practice, study, enhance comprehension, or application?

When: When during learning is it assigned and when is it due?

Who: Should you differentiate expectations or complexity?

Figure 4.10 Define What, Why, When, and Who

◆ *Terminate*: What changes can you make rather than assigning daily homework that is a busywork obligation?

> **Rather than assigning daily homework that is a stressful, busy-work obligation, empower students with occasional, meaningful, efficient, and deliberate homework that inspires ownership, curiosity, innovation or reflection to ultimately ignite a love for continuous learning.**

Figure 4.11 Occasional, Meaningful, and Deliberate Homework

◆ *Entrust*: Entrust students to self-reflect about an assignment or assessment by learning from their mistakes.

Self-reflection about assignment or assessment learning mistakes

Name: _____ Date: _____ Subject: _____

1. What was confusing? _____

2. Explain how your thinking has changed after reviewing mistakes: _____

3. Draw and explain (on the back of this) a concept or problem you struggled with:

4. Explain what changes you made based on the feedback you reviewed: _____

5. What will you do in the future to improve your understanding about a specific standard or skill?

6. How are you feeling now? _____

*Attach this reflection to your corrected assignment or assessment

Figure 4.12 Student Reflection on Learning from Mistakes

5

Learning Targets

Aligning homework with specific targets makes homework more meaningful. Homework learning targets specify the primary, essential, or relevant standards, skills, big ideas, concepts, understandings, or success criteria. Learning targets are a foundation for the creation of focused success criteria discussed in Chapters 10 and 11.

Deliberate homework learning targets focus on providing practice and feedback that lead to a deeper understanding about one or multiple primary or essential standards, skills, big ideas, themes, or concepts. The thoughtfully planned focus might be guided by one or two essential grade-level standards or skills students can practice independently and on which they can receive feedback. Major and supporting grade-level standards, or the level of importance and student readiness, should be considered when assigning homework that increases in complexity. Before reading this chapter, please take a few minutes to answer the self-assessment questions below.

Table 5.1 Self-Assessment of Current Homework Practices

	Never	Rarely	Sometimes	Often	Always
I assign homework that is busywork and not related to specific learning, skills, or standards.					
Deliberate homework learning targets focus on providing practice and feedback that lead to a deeper understanding about one or multiple primary or essential standards, skills, big ideas, themes, or concepts.					
I create options for students to practice skills they think they need to improve, based on their self-assessment of their progress and understanding.					

What

Homework expectations align with beliefs, values, and identified enduring standards deemed essential for future growth. Attention to homework learning targets can range on a continuum that includes: (1) busywork not related to specific learning, skill, or standard; (2) homework that practices a specific skill, standard, or review skills; (3) homework that practices current and recently learned skills; or (4) homework that is based on personalized differentiated learning targets.

Why

Deliberate learning targets can make homework more meaningful and can help prioritize learning decisions. Specific learning targets can also guide decisions about success criteria and exemplars. Benefits of deliberate learning targets include a clear focus on critical grade-level standards and skills, and guide exclusion of homework that does not align with primary grade-level standards and skills. Teachers who are inattentive to homework learning targets assign busywork that focuses on less important standards or skills, has too many standards or skills, or does not provide feedback linked to specific standards or skills. Potential negative impacts when one is not deliberate about learning targets include homework that is less meaningful and ineffective when not aligned with grade-level standards and skills.

How

Meaningful homework identifies the major or supporting grade-level state standards or skills being practiced. Meaningful homework should focus on one or two state standards or skills unless the review interweaves practice and previously learned information. Teachers can differentiate homework learning targets by allowing students to choose the sequence of their learning. An alternative example is unrelated to current learning but is related to grade-level skills such as math, spelling, or vocabulary. Tasks could include skill-based personalized online math, learning Latin roots, or practicing spelling words. This work could always be due on a specific day of the week and could be the only homework or a type of homework that occurs every other week.

Challenges teachers may encounter include having multiple grade-level standards and skills to cover, causing students to be hyper-focused on standards rather than a love for learning. Related topics for additional research about deliberate homework learning targets include curriculum standards and skills.

Table 5.2 Guiding Primary Question Regarding Homework Learning Targets

Guiding Primary Question	Your Response
How can you enhance alignment between your homework assignments and effective learning targets and strategies?	

The following implementation planner and reflection questions can guide discussions and potential homework improvements for learning targets.

Table 5.3 Chapter Implementation Planner for Homework Learning Targets

Topics I will ...	Responses
Investigate	
Discuss	
Reflect on	
Change	

D.E.L.I.B.E.R.A.T.E. Continuous Improvement Questions for Homework Learning Targets

The following D.E.L.I.B.E.R.A.T.E. questions can guide reflection, discussion, and professional learning by asking you to Differentiate, Explain, Learn, Implement, Bolster, Empower, Reflect, Ask, Terminate, and Entrust.

◆ *Differentiate*: Create options for students to practice skills they think they need to improve on based on the self-assessment of their progress and understanding.

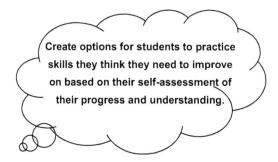

Create options for students to practice skills they think they need to improve on based on their self-assessment of their progress and understanding.

Figure 5.1 Improve Based on Self-Assessment of Progress

◆ *Explain* how five of your homework assignments identify the major or supporting grade-level standards or skills being practiced.

Meaningful homework identifies the major or supporting grade level standards or skills that are being practiced.

Figure 5.2 Major and Supporting Standards

◆ *Learn*: Identify and commit to learning about, applying, and sharing findings regarding grade-level practice opportunities related to critical learning targets.

Identify and commit to learning about, applying, and sharing findings regarding grade level practice opportunities related to critical learning targets.

Figure 5.3 Learn about Critical Learning Targets

◆ *Implement*: How will you ensure students are provided with multiple learning opportunities for every priority learning standard?

Rather than debating if students should be able to redo or correct assignments or assessments, a related solution is ensuring students are provided multiple learning opportunities for every learning standard.

Figure 5.4 Multiple Learning Opportunities

◆ *Bolster*: What homework (or learning) activities can you create to inspire a focus on skills?

What homework (or learning) activities can you create to inspire focus on skills?

Ask questions	Investigate
Define problems	Interpret data
Use models	Construct explanations
Solve problems	Design solutions
Reason	Engage in argument
Construct arguments	Evaluate
Critique reasoning	Communicate

Figure 5.5 Inspire a Focus on Skills

◆ *Empower*: What next steps will you take to empower teachers and students to explain how specific homework activities align with learning standards and enhance knowledge or skills?

Teachers and students should be able to explain how specific learning activities or homework **align with learning standards and enhance knowledge or skills.**

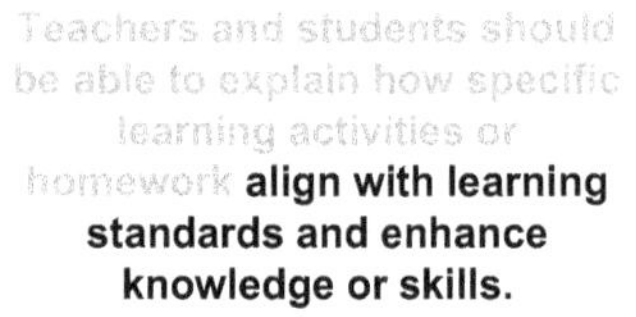

Figure 5.6 Align Homework with Standards and Skills

◆ *Reflect*: Reflect on changes that can be made so your homework aligns with a learning standard, skill, or target and is not burdensome busywork.

Homework **that does not align with a learning standard, skill or target is** burdensome busy work.

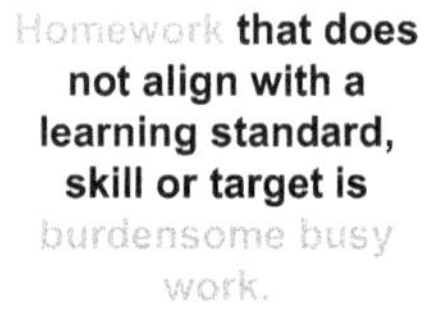

Figure 5.7 Not Burdensome Busywork

◆ *Ask*: What questions can you ask students or parents?

Homework alignment with learning targets

Step 1. What three questions can you ask students or parents to gather information regarding their understanding and alignment of learning targets?

1._____
_____
_____
2._____
_____
_____
3._____
_____
_____

Step 2. Discuss questions with colleagues.

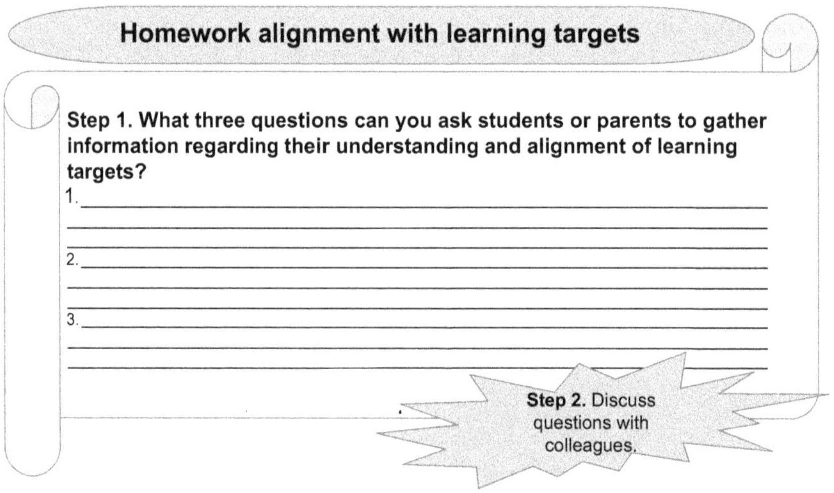

Figure 5.8 Understanding and Alignment of Learning Targets

◆ *Terminate*: Identify homework assignments and learning practices you will stop using.

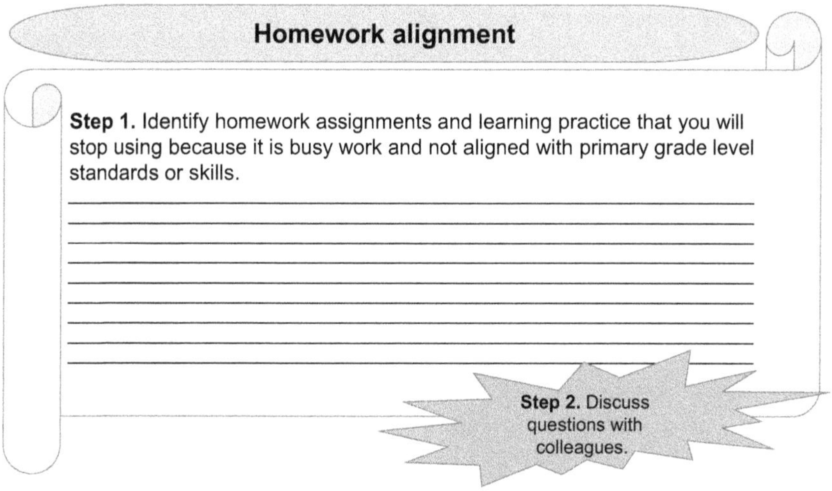

Homework alignment

Step 1. Identify homework assignments and learning practice that you will stop using because it is busy work and not aligned with primary grade level standards or skills.

_____
_____
_____
_____
_____
_____
_____
_____

Step 2. Discuss questions with colleagues.

Figure 5.9 Homework Alignment

◆ *Entrust* students to make connections between themselves and learning topics.

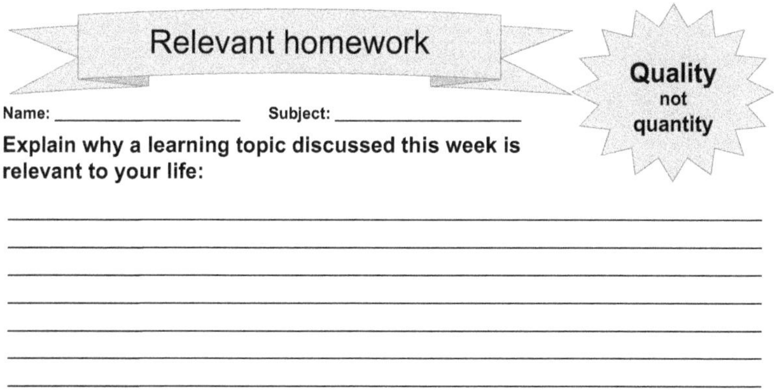

Relevant homework

Quality not quantity

Name: _____   Subject: _____

Explain why a learning topic discussed this week is relevant to your life:

_____
_____
_____
_____
_____
_____
_____

Figure 5.10 Relevant Homework

6

The Learning Mindset

The homework process should be guided by a learning mindset that focuses on teachers empowering students to be responsible, resourceful, resilient, and reflective. Carol Dweck (2007) explained why having a growth mindset enhances motivation and productivity. Aspects of a growth mindset can guide educator perspectives to empower learning in their schools.

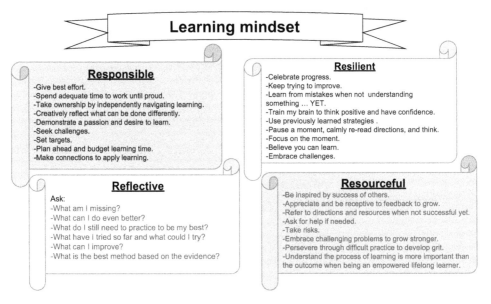

Figure 6.1 The Learning Mindset

Before reading this chapter, please take a few minutes to answer the self-assessment question below.

Table 6.1 Self-Assessment of Current Homework Practices

	Never	Rarely	Sometimes	Often	Always
I discuss and model the importance of being responsible, resilient, reflective, and resourceful.					

What

A learning mindset is a way of thinking. Educators should have a common definition of a learning mindset and be aware of potential negative and positive impacts that homework has on learning mindsets. A learning mindset should support and empower students so they can grapple in a productive learning struggle and reflectively persevere through cognitive dissonance. Teachers can make time to model and empower a learning mindset to help students reflect on goals and envision success as they continuously learn and unlearn with a growth mindset. Teachers can also empower students to recognize and appreciate the journey, mistakes, beauty, grit, productive struggle, and progress that happen during curious and reflective inquiry with a growth mindset.

Teachers who are inattentive about a learning mindset don't explicitly notice or support non-academic skills that can enhance learning and persistence. Challenges that teachers may encounter include limited focus on academic strengths rather than the whole child, as well as lack of awareness about individual strengths and needs. Related topics for additional research about a deliberate learning mindset include a growth mindset and social emotional learning (SEL).

Why

Educators should empower students, educators, and parents to be fascinated by mistakes to guide questions, reflection, change, progress, support, guidance, and differentiation. Mistakes and failures delay progress while inspiring humility, adaption, persistence, and continuous learning with a growth mindset. Mistakes and failures are teachable moments that empower reflection, learning, and adapting with a growth mindset. A learning mindset can support homework by empowering students to want to enhance understanding rather than complete an assignment or earn a high grade. A learning mindset can also enhance students' beliefs in their capacity to learn, to enable students to resiliently bounce back from adversity, and to empower agency, efficacy, persistence, and curious self-directed learning. A learning mindset can also have a positive impact on learning critical skills, empowering a love for learning, and inspiring connections to interests, passions, talents, or other topics.

A learning mindset has a social-emotional impact on stress tolerance, regulating emotions, perseverance, setting and monitoring personal goals, self-evaluating, resourcefulness, awareness of strengths, perspective taking, responsible decision making, metacognition, goal setting, solving problems, help seeking, organizational skills, self-confidence, self-efficacy, perseverance, and resiliency. The benefits of a deliberate learning mindset include enhancing self-regulation, control, empathy, persistence, and a passion to learn, grow, and build on strengths and weaknesses. Potential negative impacts when not deliberate about learning mindsets include students being unaware of strengths and helpful behaviors.

How

Teachers should create a trusting and supportive learning community in their classroom where students are expected to take risks, make mistakes, reflectively solve problems, make connections, seek assistance, and help others. Teachers can nurture, empower, support, and differentiate a learning mindset by building caring relationships. Maximizing relationships with students and colleagues empowers engagement, collaboration, and continuous learning. Modeling and supporting a learning mindset and culture in the classroom will empower students to be responsible, resilient, reflective, and resourceful while they work on their homework and as self-directed learners.

Educators can empower a learning mindset by thinking aloud in class, modeling, discussing teachable moments, and discussing attributes of characters from stories, community members, and famous people. Educators can model and empower a learning mindset by helping students to enhance the skills shown in Figure 6.2.

Empower a continuous learning mindset
by helping students enhance:

Self-confidence   Self-efficacy   Self-evaluating   Help seeking

Stress management   Regulating emotions   Perseverance

Resilience   Resourcefulness   Awareness of strengths

Perspective taking   Responsible decision making   Consequences

Metacognition   Attention regulation   Setting and monitoring   Personal goals

Solving problems   Decision making   Organizational skills

Figure 6.2 Empower a Learning Mindset

Table 6.2 Guiding Primary Questions Regarding a Homework Learning Mindset

Guiding Primary Question	Your Response
How will you model and empower a learning mindset to enhance focus on students being responsible, resilient, reflective, and resourceful?	
How will you build trusting relationships and a culture that empowers courageous continuous learning with a learning mindset?	

The following implementation planner and reflection questions can guide discussions and potential homework improvements for a learning mindset.

Table 6.3 Chapter Implementation Planner for a Homework Learning Mindset

Topics I will ...	Responses
Investigate	
Discuss	
Reflect on	
Change	

D.E.L.I.B.E.R.A.T.E. Continuous Improvement Questions for Homework Learning Mindset

The following D.E.L.I.B.E.R.A.T.E questions can guide reflection, discussion, and professional learning by asking you to Differentiate, Explain, Learn, Implement, Bolster, Empower, Reflect, Ask, Terminate, and Entrust.

◆ *Differentiate*: How will you build trusting relationships?

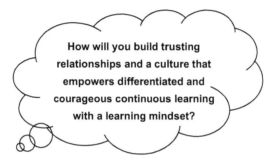

Figure 6.3 Build Trusting Relationships

◆ *Explain*: How will you model and empower a learning mindset to enhance a focus on students being responsible, resilient, reflective, and resourceful?

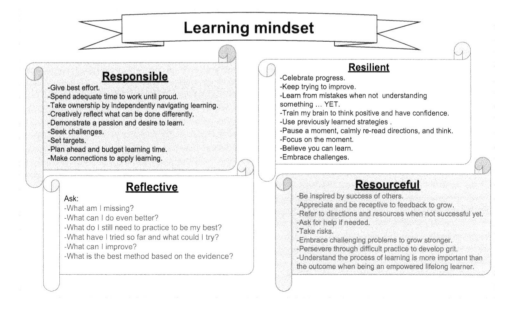

Figure 6.4 A Learning Mindset

◆ *Learn*: What can you read regarding a learning mindset or a growth mindset?

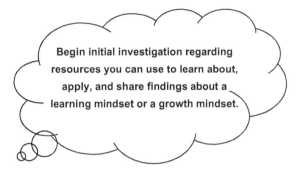

Begin initial investigation regarding resources you can use to learn about, apply, and share findings about a learning mindset or a growth mindset.

Figure 6.5 Learn More about a Growth Mindset

◆ *Implement*: How will you implement a learning mindset in your classroom, school, and school district?

**Reflectively embrace
discomfort and progress
rather than being distracted by
failure or perfection.**

Figure 6.6 Embrace Discomfort and Progress

◆ *Bolster*: How will you model, empower, and bolster a learning mindset by helping students enhance the skills below?

Empower a continuous learning mindset by helping students enhance:

Self-confidence   Self-efficacy   Self-evaluating   Help seeking

Stress management   Regulating emotions   Perseverance

Resilience   Resourcefulness   Awareness of strengths

Perspective taking   Responsible   Decision making   Consequences

Metacognition   Attention regulation   Setting and monitoring Personal goals

Solving problems   Decision making   Organizational skills

Figure 6.7 Empower a Learning Mindset

◆ *Empower*: How can you empower student confidence?

**Believe you will make a
difference for every student
and teacher, and tell them
you believe until they believe
in themselves.**

Figure 6.8 Believe You Will Make a Difference

◆ *Reflect* on ways you can empower a learning mindset, as described below, in your classroom, school, or school district in the near future.

Reflect about continuous improvement

Relationships with students and colleagues inspire learning.

Engaged learning is maximized.

What and how will you continuously
improve in your classroom, school, or
school district in the near future?

Feedback is timely and specifically guides reflection and growth.

Learners love to learn, create, collaborate, and solve problems.

**Empowered growth mindsets inspire risks, resourcefulness, and
learning from mistakes.**

Choice and voice amplifies self-direction and differentiated learning.

Teachers believe in their ability to positively affect students (efficacy).

Figure 6.9 Reflect on Continuous Improvement

◆ *Ask*: What will you ask students to empower their reflecting on and learning from failure and mistakes?

**Empower the freedom to fail by
acknowledging students and staff
who** try something new, fail,
correctly attribute failure to the right
reasons, and continue to make
changes **during the process of
continuous learning with a growth
mindset.**

Figure 6.10 Learn from Failure and Mistakes

F **Fearless**
A **Analytical**
I **Innovative**
L **Learning**
U **Until**
R **Resilience**
E **Endures**

Figure 6.11 Failure

◆ *Terminate*: What practices or behaviors will you decrease or stop?

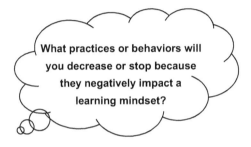

Figure 6.12 Decrease or Stop Practices or Behaviors

◆ *Entrust*: How will you entrust students to maximize the power of: What if? Why not? And I don't know yet?

Figure 6.13 Maximize the Power

Reference

Dweck, C. (2007). *Mindset: The New Psychology of Success.* New York: Ballantine.

7

Format

Homework format should deliberately align with meaningful homework purpose, learning targets, and complexity. Homework format refers to how the activity is completed; more specifically, the organization and completion options. Deliberate modifications empower ownership of homework and learning by providing trust, choice, and responsibility up front. Regardless of the five previously identified purposes, homework format typically includes one way or multiple ways to demonstrate understanding via specific questions or open-ended options and directions. Homework questions can have one correct answer, can be open-ended, or can have multiple correct answers. Questions can focus on one concept or skill or provide mixed practice to review learned skills. Format can vary by number of questions or problems as well as levels of independence. Independent activities should be able to be completed without assistance, while collaborative activities could include working with another student, explaining to someone, or teaching another person. Before reading this chapter, please take a few minutes to answer the self-assessment questions below.

Table 7.1 Self-Assessment of Current Homework Practices

	Never	Rarely	Sometimes	Often	Always
Does your homework empower students to personalize how they demonstrate their understanding by targeting students' natural curiosity to discover, create, or ask questions?					
I provide reflection opportunities to empower students to think about why they are learning and make connections with other topics, previous learning, or personal interests.					
My homework format aligns with purposes of practice, differentiation, communication, exploration, and innovation.					

What

Meaningful homework helps students to independently practice learned skills at appropriate levels of difficulty; offers choices and differentiates learning opportunities; maximizes flexibility for other responsibilities by allowing multiple days to complete; encourages connections and extensions of learning to contexts outside of the classroom; welcomes feedback from teachers and students; offers opportunities for reflection, goal setting, and innovation; recognizes accuracy as a reason for recording this as a responsibility grade rather than an academic grade; and keys in on enhancing proficiency, accuracy, speed, or fluency. Format can also include there being one way to finish the homework, provide a few choices, or create multiple choices for students.

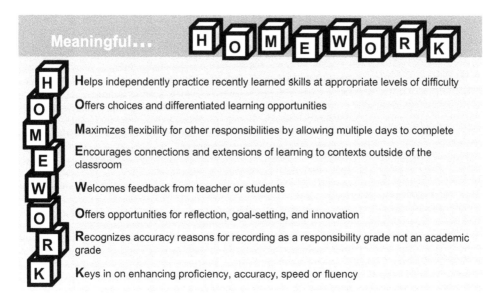

Figure 7.1 Meaningful Homework

A deliberate homework format can empower students to personalize how they demonstrate their understanding by targeting students' natural curiosity to discover, create, or ask questions. A deliberate homework format includes open-ended questions that encourage inquiry and making connections. It can also empower students by providing choices regarding which questions they answer or how they demonstrate their understanding with meaningful opportunities for practice, communication, exploring, innovation, and differentiation. Choice activities empower making connections to enhance relevance, leveraging strengths, self-directed learning, or demonstrating understanding in creative ways. Students could have a choice about how long they work on homework based on their progress and confidence. A great example of differentiated, independent, and meaningful homework is providing students with multiple days to choose and complete one or several activities from a list and to demonstrate their knowledge, skills, and abilities.

Teachers should provide reflection opportunities to empower students to think about why they are learning and make connections with other topics, previous learning, or personal interests. Teachers can differentiate the format with concise and open-ended homework that empowers deliberate practice, reflection, or making of connections. Unmindful homework formats can be monotonous for students who understand the skill or concept, and it may be too difficult for those struggling to understand the skill, concept, strategy, or completion options. Homework should include beneficial practice rather than unrelated art or meaningless waste of time work such as word searches.

Why

A deliberate homework format empowers choice, voice, engagement, ownership, and continuous learning with a growth mindset. Benefits of a deliberate homework format include a variety of meaningful learning opportunities that align with a deliberate purpose and inspire engagement and a love for learning. Challenges teachers may encounter include finding time to create, find, or plan, and changing activities from previous years.

One potential negative about a deliberate homework format includes an equity challenge regarding students' access to resources for support or projects. A second potential negative is the teacher finding or creating too many unique activities that students may not understand the routine or process.

How

Deliberate homework formats can be created by reflecting on questions. How will you inspire curiosity and student ownership by deliberately making homework more meaningful, flexible, personalized, or open-ended? How consistent are the homework formats for your grade level, school, or school district? Rather than homework, what will students be asked to think about to empower reflection and higher order thinking? Do all students have equitable resources? What if homework is focused more on creating questions to empower learning the next day? Are there specific students who would benefit from targeted concise homework to meet a deliberate need? Is there a student who you can modify practice opportunities for in school and not assign homework because there is minimal or no home support? Related topics for additional research about the deliberate homework format include creativity, innovation, and motivation.

Deliberate homework formats empower students to do a variety of targeted and concise thinking. Figure 7.2 illustrates examples that range from self-assessing prior knowledge to self-directed learning. Figure 7.3 can guide reflection on additional format options for reasonable and meaningful homework.

Deliberate homework formats
Empower students to...

~Self-assess prior knowledge ~Preview upcoming learning ~Watch a brief video ~Learn new vocabulary ~Create questions ~Empower curiosity ~Revisit prior learning ~Answer open-ended questions	~Explain a strategy ~What are you confused about? ~Prioritize most important understandings ~Synthesize understanding ~Make Connections ~Reflect ~How did you grow today? ~Identify one success ~Make sense of learning ~Apply to a different context ~Choose how ~Ask questions ~Justify why	~Investigate ~Demonstrate ~Create ~Explore ~Teach someone ~Creatively build ~Set goals ~Reflect about progress ~Self-directed learning ~Write about themself ~Read about the importance of sleep

Figure 7.2 Deliberate Homework Formats

Occasional, deliberate, and efficient homework reflection questions

Create occasional, deliberate, and efficient homework by answering the reflection questions below and then discussing with fellow educators, implementation options for three of your responses.

What changes can be made to your homework that enhances opportunities for:

1. Less frequent homework: _____
2. Choice: _____
3. Multiple days to complete activities: _____
4. Differentiation: _____
5. Reflection or goal setting: _____
6. Making connections or extending learning: _____
_____
7. Deliberate and meaningful independent practice: _____
_____
8. Innovation: _____

Figure 7.3 Occasional, Deliberate, and Efficient Homework Reflection Questions

Table 7.2 Guiding Primary Question Regarding Homework Format

Guiding Primary Question	Your Response
How can you ensure that the format for every homework assignment has a meaningful purpose, appropriate complexity, and aligns with a pertinent learning target?	

The following implementation planner and reflection questions can guide discussions and potential homework improvements for format.

Table 7.3 Chapter Implementation Planner for Homework Format

Topics I will ...	Responses
Investigate	
Discuss	
Reflect on	
Change	

D.E.L.I.B.E.R.A.T.E. Continuous Improvement Questions for Homework Format

The following D.E.L.I.B.E.R.A.T.E questions can guide reflection, discussion, and professional learning by asking you to Differentiate, Explain, Learn, Implement, Bolster, Empower, Reflect, Ask, Terminate, and Entrust.

◆ *Differentiate*: How can you differentiate homework formats to meet the needs of different learners?

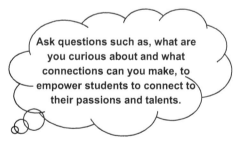

Ask questions such as, what are you curious about and what connections can you make, to empower students to connect to their passions and talents.

Figure 7.4 Connect to Passions and Talents

What would the benefits be if you differentiated student focus by assigning gratitude homework three times a year?

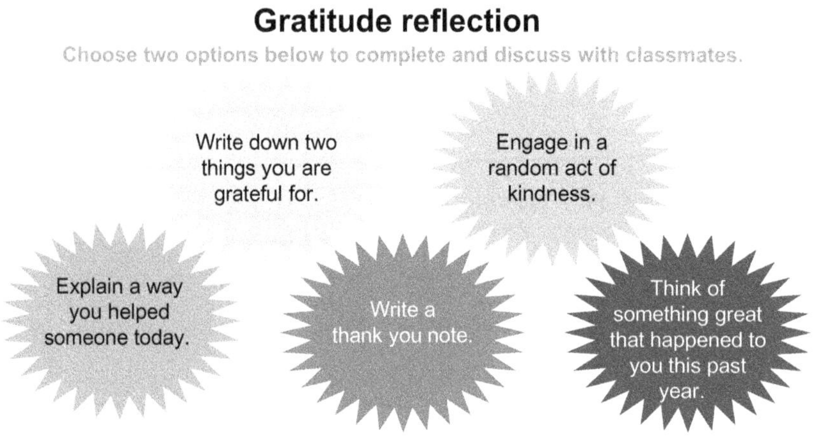

Gratitude reflection

Choose two options below to complete and discuss with classmates.

Write down two
things you are
grateful for.

Engage in a
random act of
kindness.

Explain a way
you helped
someone today.

Write a
thank you note.

Think of
something great
that happened to
you this past
year.

Figure 7.5 Gratitude Reflection

◆ *Explain*: Choose homework problems or questions to answer and then explain how your practice improved your understanding. Select one completed assignment that is the best example of learning. In the space below explain to your parents what you are proud of.

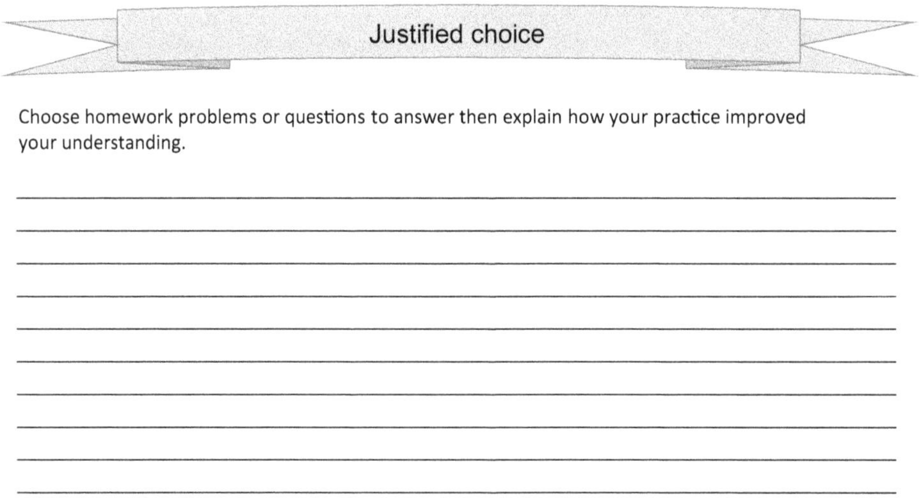

Justified choice

Choose homework problems or questions to answer then explain how your practice improved your understanding.

_____
_____
_____
_____
_____
_____
_____
_____
_____
_____
_____
_____

Figure 7.6 Justified Choice

Proud reflection

Quality
not
quantity

Name: _____ Subject: _____

Select one completed assignment that is the best example of recent learning.
Explain to your parents in the space below what you are proud of.

_____
_____
_____
_____
_____
_____
_____

Figure 7.7 Proud Reflection

◆ *Learn*: Identify and commit to learning about homework format.

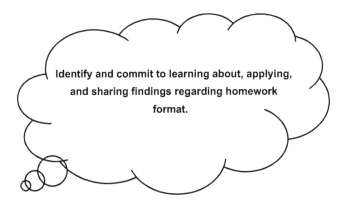

Identify and commit to learning about, applying,
and sharing findings regarding homework
format.

Figure 7.8 Learn About Homework Format

◆ *Implement*: How can the math reflection homework described below
be used with your students?

Math reflection homework

Name: _____   Date: _____

1. A brief summary of math problem solving process practiced this week:	
2. A mistake I learned from this week is:	
3. Reflection about problem solving, creativity, collaboration, or quality of my work this week:	
4. Behavior or academic goal for upcoming week:	

Figure 7.9 Math Reflection Homework

◆ *Bolster*: How can you bolster homework format options from the examples noted below? When can you implement occasional innovation homework as explained below?

Occasional innovation homework

Educators recognize the importance of empowering student innovation and curiosity. However, learning time in the classroom can be limited and meaningful homework continues to be a debated topic. Use this planning sheet to guide inspiring innovative learning in the classroom and at home.

1. Classroom activity: Explain parameters for a self-directed innovative learning project that could be guided by expectations for a makerspace activity, Genius Hour opportunity, or Passion, Wonder Day or Wonder Week project.
2. Classroom activity: Guide and provide feedback regarding topic selection.

3. Homework: Complete planning sheet to identify topic, background information, inquiry questions, and resources.

4. Classroom activity: Provide class time for students to begin self-directed innovative learning project.

5. Homework: Research and read about topics selected for self-directed innovative learning project.

6. Classroom activity: Empower students to collaboratively reflect and revise self-directed projects, finish projects and start planning class presentations.

7. Homework: Work on class presentation, complete reflection questions, and self-assess project via rubric.

8. Classroom Activity: Present self-directed project to class and provide feedback on classmates' projects.

Figure 7.10 Occasional Innovation Homework

What pre-learning homework could enhance students' learning?

Pre-learning homework

Write down 3 things you know about the topic we
will learn about tomorrow and one question.

Tomorrow's topic is: _____

Figure 7.11 Pre-Learning Homework

What additional ways can you help students study for upcoming assessments?

Connect meaningful homework
with learning and assessments
by allowing students to use one
page of their homework notes
during the assessment.

Figure 7.12 Assessment Notes

◆ *Empower*: What questions can you ask to generate curiosity and a love for learning over the summer?

**For continuous improvement, what
will you learn, read, research,
improve, create, or reflect about
this summer?**

Goal: _____
_____
Success Criteria: _____

Figure 7.13 Summer Reflection

Create a concise and meaningful homework choice menu and share it with colleagues and your professional learning community on Twitter.

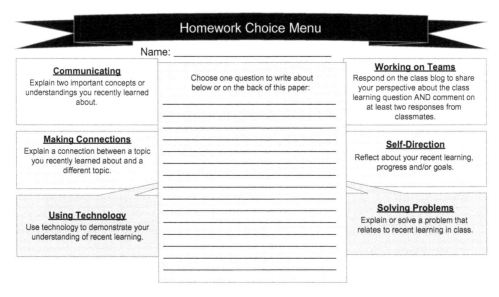

Figure 7.14 Homework Choice Menu

◆ *Reflect*: Reflect, connect, question, and connect. How does recent learning inform future thinking?

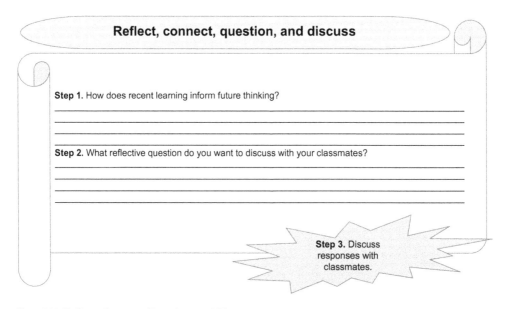

Figure 7.15 Reflect, Connect, Question, and Discuss

When and how will you use these homework reflections and self-assessments?

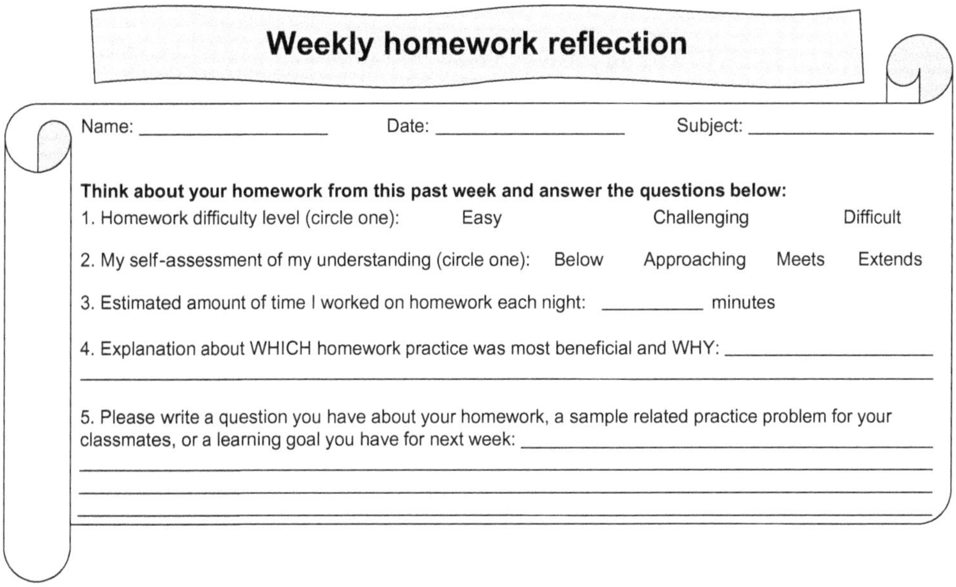

Weekly homework reflection

Name: _____   Date: _____   Subject: _____

Think about your homework from this past week and answer the questions below:

1. Homework difficulty level (circle one):   Easy   Challenging   Difficult

2. My self-assessment of my understanding (circle one):   Below   Approaching   Meets   Extends

3. Estimated amount of time I worked on homework each night: _____ minutes

4. Explanation about WHICH homework practice was most beneficial and WHY: _____
_____

5. Please write a question you have about your homework, a sample related practice problem for your classmates, or a learning goal you have for next week: _____
_____
_____
_____

Figure 7.16 Weekly Homework Reflection

◆ *Ask*: Empower discussions with parents and classmates by asking the following questions. What did you learn today that you can teach someone else? The result could be that parents ask their child this question rather than: What is your homework tonight?

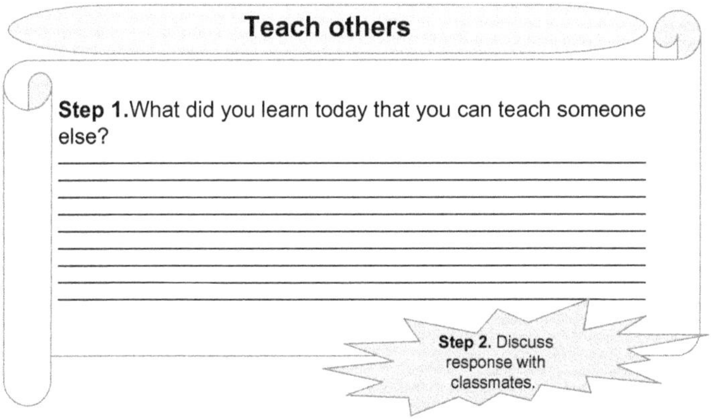

Teach others

Step 1. What did you learn today that you can teach someone else?
_____
_____
_____
_____
_____
_____
_____

Step 2. Discuss response with classmates.

Figure 7.17 Teach Others

How would the question below benefit your students?

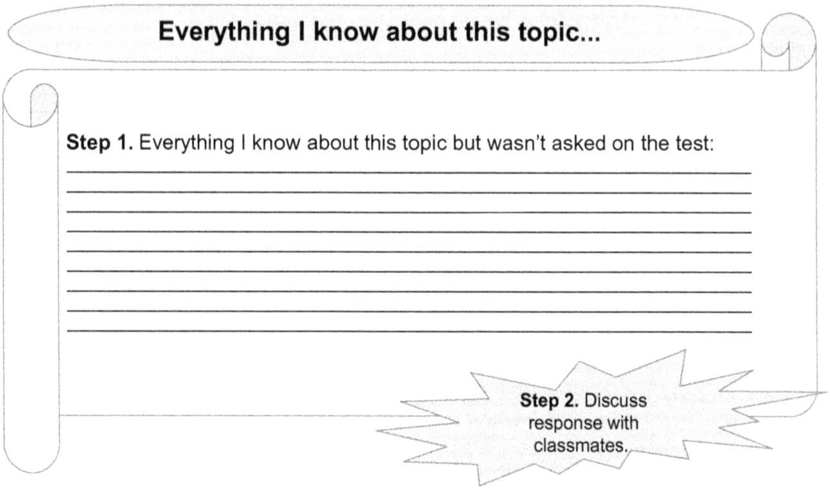

Everything I know about this topic...

Step 1. Everything I know about this topic but wasn't asked on the test:

Step 2. Discuss response with classmates.

Figure 7.18 Everything I Know About This Topic

◆ *Terminate*: Explain three examples in which you plan to assign one or two quality homework questions or practice problems rather than multiple, mediocre, low level, less meaningful, or unnecessary questions or problems.

Assign 1 or 2 quality homework questions or practice problems rather than multiple, mediocre, low level, less meaningful, or unnecessary questions or problems.

Quality not quantity

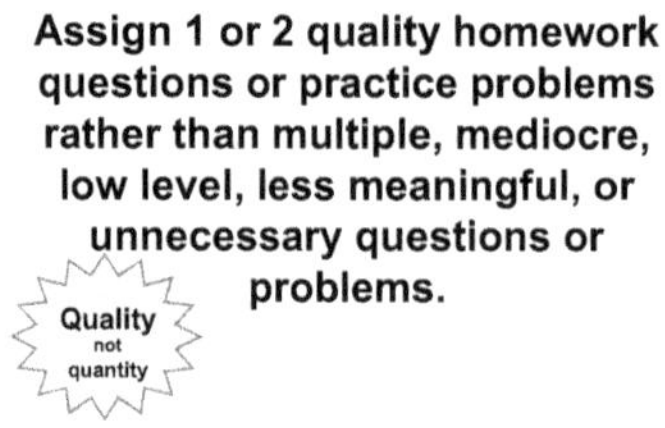

Figure 7.19 Quality Homework

◆ *Entrust*: How can you enhance student choice?

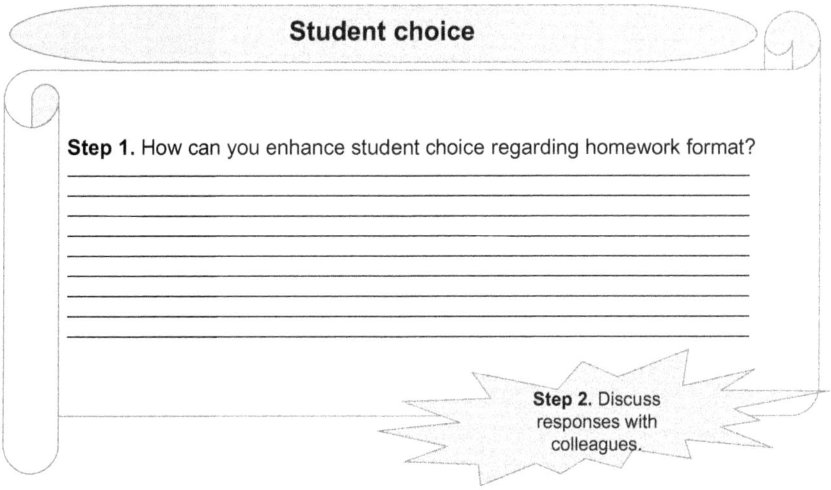

Student choice

Step 1. How can you enhance student choice regarding homework format?
_____
_____
_____
_____
_____
_____
_____
_____
_____

Step 2. Discuss responses with colleagues.

Figure 7.20 Student Choice

8

Sequence

A general sequence of teaching and learning as well as a sequence specifically related to homework assignments are both pertinent for deliberate homework. The broad learning sequence and process include instruction, guided practice, independent practice, support, and assessment. Homework assignments happen in the instructional sequence after successful independent practice. An alternative sequence is pre-learning or previewing homework activities that create a foundation for building future learning. A second alternative is modifying the sequence by empowering students to skip content when they demonstrate proficiency in a formal or informal pre-assessment. Before reading this chapter, please take a few minutes to answer the self-assessment questions below.

Table 8.1 Self-Assessment of Current Homework Practices

	Never	Rarely	Sometimes	Often	Always
I divide learning into phases so homework complexity levels increase after students demonstrate proficiency.					
I ensure students have had meaningful guided and independent practice at school so frequency and amount of homework are both reasonable.					
I empower students to choose how they practice learning a common learning target.					
I have a process that allows students to skip content when they demonstrate proficiency on a formal or informal pre-assessment.					

What

Deliberately planned homework aligns with purpose and student needs and includes available guidance and support if students are unsuccessful. Teachers must ensure that complex questions are not inappropriately asked before students are ready for them. If deliberately planned homework is the additional practice of a skill, process, or standard, teachers must ensure students have had meaningful guided and independent practice at school so the frequency and amount of homework are both reasonable.

Teachers should think about modifications that need to be made regarding the sequence of homework questions on individual assignments as well as related assignments. Learning should evolve from concrete to more abstract by building a foundation with opportunities to draw, see models, and make. An inappropriate homework sequence is not logical and has a negative impact on learning. Independent practice is inappropriately assigned before students demonstrate understanding and/or problem solving abilities. Lack of success can impact the amount of time spent on homework and can enhance frustration. Related topics for additional research include a deliberate homework sequence, learning theory, scaffolding support, and scope and sequences.

Why

A properly aligned sequence can enhance the other 11 homework character-istics, while a misaligned sequence or missing characteristics can diminish effectiveness. A deliberate homework sequence should be guided by deci-sions about complexity and learning targets to enhance the effectiveness of differentiated homework. Benefits of a deliberate sequence include having learning opportunities that logically build from foundational skills and align with student needs, enhance meaning, and align with a defined purpose. Potential negative impacts when not deliberate about a sequence include homework being too easy or too complicated, incoherent, or less relevant, resulting in decreased engagement. Challenges teachers may encounter include planning collaboratively and being guided by a scope and sequence that aligns with state standards and student, school, and school district needs.

How

There are a variety of ways teachers can leverage learning by being cognizant of a sequence of activities or questions. Figure 8.1 shows a guiding model to sequen-tially modifying complexity by dividing learning and homework into four phases that focus on different skills and levels of complexity. The four phases of sequential learning encourage teachers to focus on different skills and levels of complexity to empower pre-learning, learning, practice, and application. The

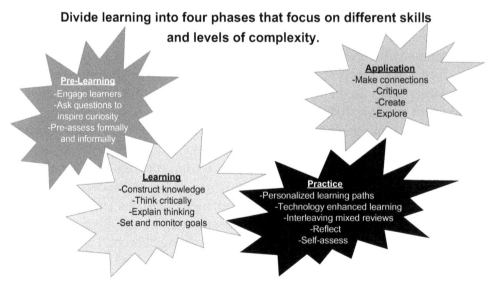

Figure 8.1 Four Phases of Sequential Complexity

first phase of pre-learning engages learners by empowering them to ask questions to enhance curiosity and formally or informally pre-assess. The second phase of learning empowers students to construct knowledge, think critically, explain thinking, and set and monitor goals. The third phase of practice empowers students to reflect, self-assess, monitor practice, personalize learning paths, communicate, interleave mixed reviews, and enhance learning with technology. The fourth and final phase of application empowers making connections, creating, critiquing, exploring, and communicating about topics of interest. This model addresses a potential equity concern regarding access if, for example, lower ability students are rarely encouraged to apply learning by making connections, critiquing, creating, or exploring. This model empowers all students at different stages of learning. All students ask questions and pre-assess their understanding during pre-learning, just as all students have personalized learning paths that empower reflection and self-assessment during the practice stage.

Teachers can empower student ownership of the sequence for learning and homework practice in a variety of ways. Examples include empowering student choice, differentiating, and/or enhancing complexity when students demonstrate proficiency as well as skipping content if students demonstrate understanding, choose the process for a common learning target, choose how they practice learning a common learning target, or select a practice based on their specific needs. Teachers can also personalize paths by personalizing the sequence of assignments and sequence of difficulty within assignments. Feedback can also be sequenced to empower prioritization of a sequence to avoid making students feel overwhelmed by focusing on the one improvement they should make next to help guide their improvement and help them "catch-up" with classmates. Figure 8.2 provides learning sequence options that teachers can infuse into the homework process.

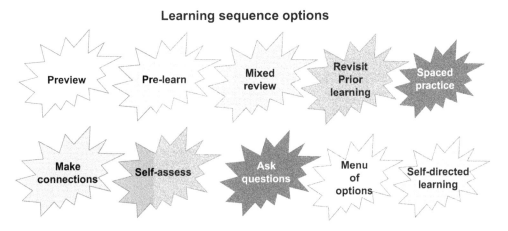

Figure 8.2 Learning Sequence Options

Table 8.2 Guiding Primary Question Regarding Homework Sequence

Guiding Primary Question	Your Response
What modifications need to be made regarding the sequence of homework questions on individual assignments as well as related assignments?	

The following implementation planner and reflection questions can guide discussions and potential homework improvements for a sequence.

Table 8.3 Chapter Implementation Planner for Homework Sequence

Topics I will ...	Responses
Investigate	
Discuss	
Reflect on	
Change	

D.E.L.I.B.E.R.A.T.E. Continuous Improvement Questions for Homework Sequence

The following D.E.L.I.B.E.R.A.T.E questions can guide reflection, discussion, and professional learning by asking you to Differentiate, Explain, Learn, Implement, Bolster, Empower, Reflect, Ask, Terminate, and Entrust.

◆ *Differentiate*: What are some ways you can flip learning so students read or listen to background information as homework before new information is taught to them?

Pre-learning homework

Step 1. What are some ways you can flip learning so students read or listen to background information as homework before new information is taught to them?

Step 2. Gather feedback from students, colleagues, and parents.

Figure 8.3 Pre-Learning Homework

◆ *Explain* modifications that need to be made to empower students to discuss and practice complex problems.

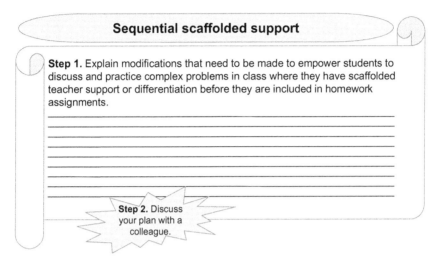

Figure 8.4 Sequential Scaffolded Support

◆ *Learn*: Begin initial investigation regarding resources for discovering learning progressions and sequences.

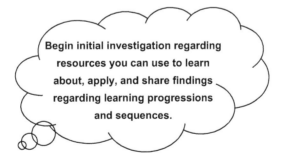

Figure 8.5 Learning Progressions and Sequences

◆ *Implement*: How can you enhance homework learning sequence options?

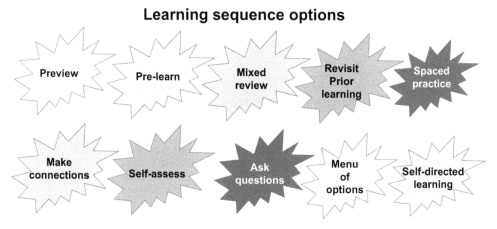

Figure 8.6 Learning Sequence Options

♦ *Bolster*: How can you bolster opportunities for student choice?

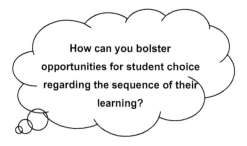

Figure 8.7 Bolster Choice of Sequence

♦ *Empower*: How will you modify the sequence of homework?

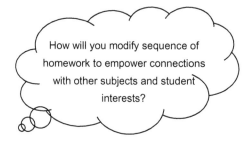

Figure 8.8 Modify Sequence to Empower Connections

◆ *Reflect*: What questions can you ask students?

Proficiency reflection

Step 1. What questions can you ask students to empower reflection about their current proficiency on learning progressions or standards?

1. _____

2. _____

3. _____

Step 2. Discuss questions with colleagues.

Figure 8.9 Proficiency Reflection

◆ *Ask*: How will you check for understanding?

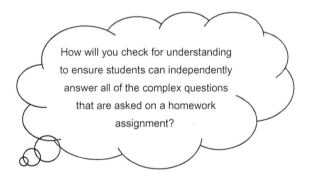

How will you check for understanding to ensure students can independently answer all of the complex questions that are asked on a homework assignment?

Figure 8.10 Check for Understanding

◆ *Terminate*: What steps will you take to check for understanding?

Figure 8.11 Demonstrate Understanding

◆ *Entrust*: How will you entrust students to have choice?

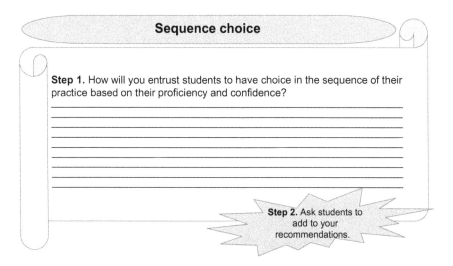

Figure 8.12 Sequence Choice

Information from the previous five chapters can collectively define whether your homework assignments are meaningful. Table 8.4 can be used to evaluate how meaningful any homework assignment is, based on the characteristics discussed in this book. You can evaluate homework by writing a checkmark under reasonable or unreasonable for each criteria. Modifications for some or all students include differentiating, enhancing, decreasing, or not assigning parts or all of the homework.

Table 8.4 Meaningful Homework Criteria

	Criteria	**Reasonable**	**Unreasonable**
Purpose	I can explain benefits for assigning this homework assignment in a way that is …		
	I thought of possible intended and unintended messages this homework assignment communicates to students and parents in a way that is …		
	Before assigning this homework I communicated what the learning purpose was for the homework assignment in a way that was …		
	My homework purposes of practice, differentiation, communication, exploration, and innovation guided my homework decisions in a way that was …		
	This homework enhances students' passion for curiosity and learning in a way that is …		
	This homework is deliberately connected to classroom teaching as a means to support and enhance learning in a way that is …		
Targets	Deliberate homework learning targets for this assignment provide practice and feedback that will lead to a deeper understanding about one or multiple primary or essential standards, skills, big ideas, themes, or concepts in a way that is …		
	This homework includes options for students to practice skills they think they need to improve on based on their self-assessment of their progress and understanding in a way that is …		

(Continued)

Table 8.4 (Continued)

	Criteria	Reasonable	Unreasonable
Mindset	I discussed and modeled the importance of being responsible, resilient, reflective, and resourceful before this homework in a way that is ...		
Format	The format for this homework assignment has a meaningful purpose, appropriate complexity, and aligns with a pertinent learning target in a way that is ...		
	The format for this homework assignment aligns with purposes of practice, differentiation, communication, exploration, and innovation in a way that is ...		
Sequence	The sequence of questions on this homework as well as related assignments is ...		
	I divided learning into phases so homework complexity levels increased after students demonstrate proficiency in a way that was ...		
	I ensured students had meaningful guided and independent practice at school so frequency and amount of homework are ...		
	I empowered students to choose how they practiced learning a common learning target in a way that was ...		

SECTION

III

Informative Homework

Deliberate homework should be reasonable, meaningful, **informative**, and consistent.

Figure S.3 Informative homework is deliberate about

9

Communication

Informative homework is an aspect of deliberate homework that is defined by communication, feedback, and grading criteria. General homework communication will be discussed in this chapter, and feedback and grading criteria will be discussed in subsequent chapters. Homework communication includes general expectations for submitting homework assignments and their specific directions. Communication for individual homework assignments explain directions, due date, the grading process, and grading criteria. Before reading this chapter, please take a few minutes to answer the self-assessment questions below.

Table 9.1 Self-Assessment of Current Homework Practices

	Never	Rarely	Sometimes	Often	Always
I gather feedback from parents and students about my homework communication to inform potential improvement.					
I differentiate homework communication based on the varying needs of the students and their parents.					

What

Deliberate respectful communication about homework builds a trusting and collaborative community of learners by specifying the purpose, explaining clear directions, and previewing homework. Written directions and due dates are also included in the students' assignment notebook or planner. Strategic thinking and communication about what materials are needed to complete concise homework empower students to bring home necessary materials rather than carrying supplies in their backpack that are not needed. Deliberate communication includes making time after guided practice to verify understanding and accuracy of work, to answer questions, and to clarify expectations. Teachers with deliberate communication gather feedback from students and parents regarding the amount of time typically spent on homework and studying, the perceived appropriateness of the difficulty level, and what could be enhanced to make the homework more meaningful and manageable. Teachers can differentiate homework purpose through multiple formats and more student-to-teacher options. Insufficient communication about homework results in lack of clarity, timeliness, and/or complete details. Challenges teachers may encounter include finding or creating a format and process for quality two-way communication. Related topics for additional research about deliberate homework communication include leadership and empathy.

Why

Parents and students should understand homework directions, success criteria, and that the grade counts as a behavior grade for responsibility rather than an academic grade for the subject. Deliberate homework communicates a shared understanding of what, how, and when to do it. Informative homework includes an explanation of the purpose of the homework to make the learning and practice more meaningful. Benefits of deliberate communication include transparency, directness, and controlling the narrative. Potential negative impacts when not being deliberate about communication include students and parents being unaware of expectations or success criteria.

How

Informative homework communication happens before the assignment, after guided practice, and after the assignment, as Figure 9.1 illustrates.

Communication before homework can happen via general expectations listed in a parent handbook, newsletter, or email. Communication during the homework process explains directions, due dates, and how to independently use resources as needed. Communication after homework includes gathering and sharing feedback, to be discussed in Chapter 10, and grading, discussed in Chapter 11.

Clearly communicate homework

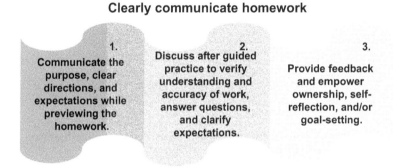

Figure 9.1 Clearly Communicate Homework

Table 9.2 Guiding Primary Question Regarding Homework Communication

Guiding Primary Question	Your Response
How can you verify that your students can confidently understand and explain the homework directions and purpose?	

The following implementation planner and reflection questions can guide discussions and potential homework improvements for communication.

Table 9.3 Chapter Implementation Planner for Homework Communication

Topics I will ...	Responses
Investigate	
Discuss	
Reflect on	
Change	

D.E.L.I.B.E.R.A.T.E. Continuous Improvement Questions for Homework Communication

The following D.E.L.I.B.E.R.A.T.E questions can guide reflection, discussion, and professional learning by asking you to Differentiate, Explain, Learn, Implement, Bolster, Empower, Reflect, Ask, Terminate, and Entrust.

◆ *Differentiate*: Specify how you will differentiate homework communication based on the varying needs of your students and their parents.

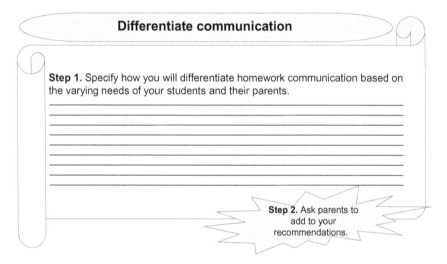

Figure 9.2 Differentiate Communication

◆ *Explain* how you will improve one of the communication phases summarized below.

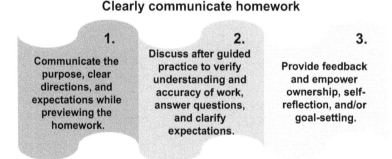

Figure 9.3 Clearly Communicate Homework

◆ *Learn* from students what guidance will help them effectively and confidently to study for assessments.

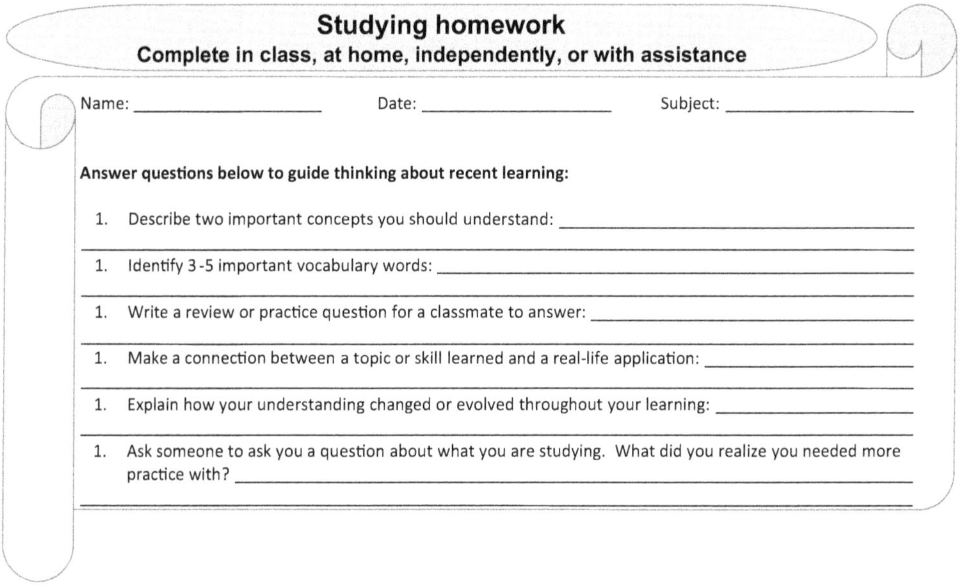

Studying homework
Complete in class, at home, independently, or with assistance

Name: _____   Date: _____   Subject: _____

Answer questions below to guide thinking about recent learning:

1. Describe two important concepts you should understand: _____

1. Identify 3-5 important vocabulary words: _____

1. Write a review or practice question for a classmate to answer: _____

1. Make a connection between a topic or skill learned and a real-life application: _____

1. Explain how your understanding changed or evolved throughout your learning: _____

1. Ask someone to ask you a question about what you are studying. What did you realize you needed more practice with? _____

Figure 9.4 Studying Homework

◆ *Implement*: Empower self-directed and confident practice.

Empower self-directed and confident practice by clearly communicating homework guidance about topics such as: what students should do if they don't understand part of the homework, what the maximum amount of time is that students should be working on a homework assignment before they stop and explain what their challenges are in writing to the teacher, and what resources will they need.

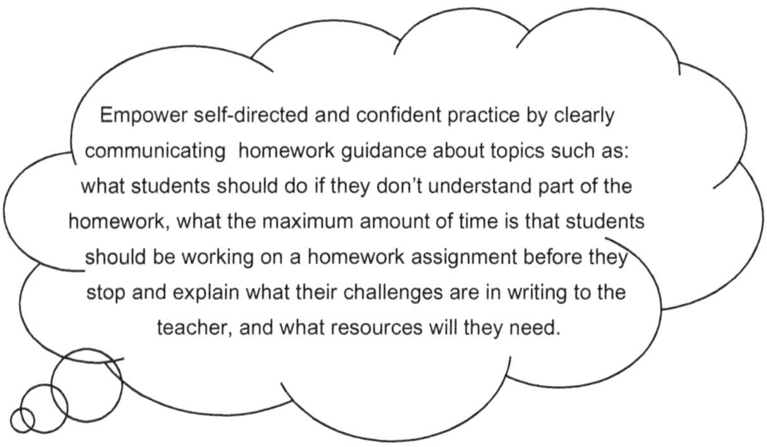

Figure 9.5 Self-Directed and Confident Practice

◆ *Bolster*: How can you help your students enhance their planning and organization skills for homework and studying?

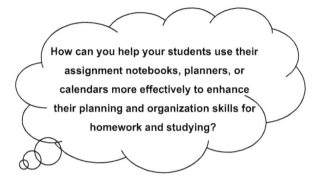

How can you help your students use their assignment notebooks, planners, or calendars more effectively to enhance their planning and organization skills for homework and studying?

Figure 9.6 Planning and Organizational Skills

◆ *Empower* students to talk with their parents.

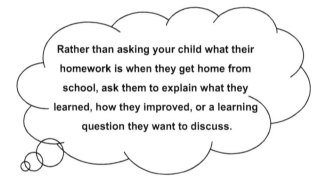

Rather than asking your child what their homework is when they get home from school, ask them to explain what they learned, how they improved, or a learning question they want to discuss.

Figure 9.7 Explain Learning

◆ *Reflect* on ways you can gather and analyze information so you can improve how your students and their parents understand homework expectations, deadlines, and feedback.

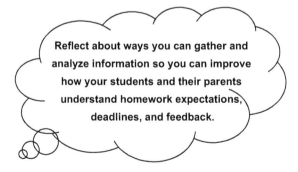

Reflect about ways you can gather and analyze information so you can improve how your students and their parents understand homework expectations, deadlines, and feedback.

Figure 9.8 Understanding

◆ *Explain* why this reflection homework would be beneficial for your students.

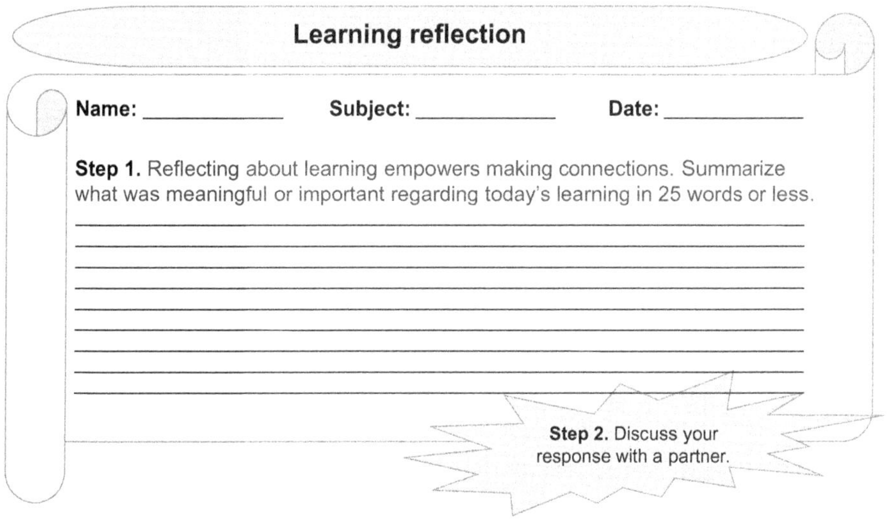

Learning reflection

Name: _____   Subject: _____   Date: _____

Step 1. Reflecting about learning empowers making connections. Summarize what was meaningful or important regarding today's learning in 25 words or less.
_____
_____
_____
_____
_____
_____
_____
_____

Step 2. Discuss your response with a partner.

Figure 9.9 Learning Reflection

◆ *Ask* your students what changes should be made to ensure their occasional independent practice or studying homework is more meaningful, concise, efficient, and deliberate. Create monthly parent homework that asks for parent feedback about the benefits and challenges with the homework.

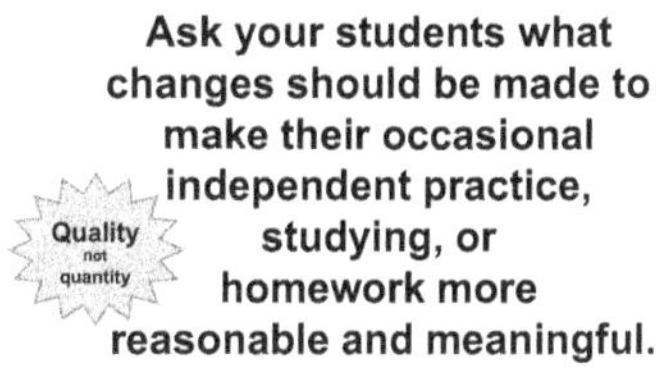

Ask your students what changes should be made to make their occasional independent practice, studying, or homework more reasonable and meaningful.

Quality not quantity

Figure 9.10 Ask

◆ *Terminate*: What ineffective communication formats will you terminate or enhance?

Communication

Step 1. How will you gather information to better understand which ineffective communication formats you will terminate or enhance?

Step 2. Discuss your response with a colleague.

Figure 9.11 Communication

◆ *Entrust* students to teach their parents via the template below and then reflect on the process with a classmate.

Weekly teach your parent homework

Name: _____ Date: _____ Subject: _____

Think about your learning from this past week and answer the questions below:
1. Identify a skill, standard or topic you learned about this week: _____

2. Explain or teach the identified skill, standard or topic to your parent.
3. Explain how this learning relates to the real world.
4. Self-assess your explanations (circle one): Below Approaching Meets Extends

5. Ask your parent to summarize their understanding of your explanations then assess your parent's understanding (circle one): Below Approaching Meets Extends
6. Describe a personal goal for using this skill, standard or topic this year: _____

7. Describe one question your parent had about the identified skill, standard or topic: _____

Figure 9.12 Weekly Teach-Your-Parent Homework

10

Feedback

Feedback and grading are meaningful parts of the homework process that occur once it is turned in. Feedback can accompany a grade or it can be given without a grade. Feedback is discussed in this book before grading as it could empower more change if timely and specific. Deliberate homework grading criteria is more meaningful and informative when communicated clearly within a process that includes feedback.

Teachers should provide meaningful, timely, actionable, understandable feedback about completed homework assignments. Homework feedback should empower learning progress and guide reflection to connect with prior learning, encourage new ideas, and inspire changes for future learning. Homework feedback connected to success criteria empowers ownership, self-reflection, goal-setting, and/or continuous improvement. Before reading this chapter, please take a few minutes to answer the self-assessment questions below.

Table 10.1 Self-Assessment of Current Homework Practices

	Never	Rarely	Sometimes	Often	Always
I write timely homework feedback.					
I empower students to provide timely homework feedback to peers.					
I connect homework feedback with success criteria.					
I gather feedback while reviewing homework to inform future teaching.					

What

Deliberate communication and feedback should happen frequently between and among teachers, students, and parents. Verbal praise empowers confidence, recognizes strengths and progress, builds relationships and a culture of learning, and empowers confidence, courage, resilience, continuous improvement, and a growth mindset. Academically focused feedback occurs during the learning process and includes questions or suggestions that elicit subsequent student action regarding where students are on a specific learning progression. Teachers should provide specific, timely, and actionable feedback and empower productive struggle, perseverance, creative problem solving, questioning, continuous learning, and a growth mindset. Additionally, teachers should know their learners, when to provide feedback, and what type of feedback to provide. Teachers should also provide time to act on the feedback, help students understand that revisions are part of the learning and growing process, and empower them to learn from others. Objective feedback should be focused on the task connected to the success criteria and learning target rather than the student. To maximize the power of feedback, teachers must look for patterns, understand where students are on learning progressions, and empower them to act on the feedback.

Along with teacher-to-student feedback, a deliberate process includes feedback from student to teacher about misconceptions and engagement, and teacher reflection about student work to plan future teaching, learning, modifications, and supports. Teachers can differentiate homework feedback by knowing students, connecting to student needs, and personalizing feedback. Challenges teachers may encounter include timeliness, amount of time to provide quality feedback, and empowering students to use feedback. Insufficient feedback is when homework is not shared, meaningful, timely, actionable, and/or understandable.

Why

Deliberate homework feedback empowers beliefs, actions, and skills. It empowers beliefs regarding confidence, courage, ownership, resilience, curiosity, and continuous improvement with a growth mindset. It empowers actions such as productive struggle, perseverance, creative problem solving, questioning, reflection, self-assessment, thinking, change, listening, acting on feedback, and continuous learning with a growth mindset. It also empowers skills such as resilience, critical thinking, creativity, curiosity, and making connections. Deliberate homework feedback can empower students to self-reflect, peer critique, make improvements, and update their online progress chart, goals, and progress. It maximizes the power and benefits of feedback and makes homework more meaningful and impactful. The benefits of deliberate feedback include clearly guiding the next steps. Potential negative effects of not being deliberate about feedback include being too late to fix a potential problem, students having less focus, or students being overwhelmed and not knowing where to start.

How

Such a culture emphasizes feedback over grading and involves students in the feedback process. Feedback should build on the foundation of providing help from a trusting and caring collaborator who empowers self-assessment and continuous improvement in a safe culture. A culture of feedback empowers students to appreciate the journey, mistakes, and grit that can happen during continuous learning through a growth mindset and to recognize that errors provide opportunities for feedback and learning. Teachable moments regarding homework can occur when teachers check for understanding, listen to students' questions, notice trends for one or multiple students, and ask questions to empower students to reflect on an error.

Feedback should be part of every independent practice activity. However, it can be provided by the teacher, a classmate, or via self-reflection on the work. Deliberate homework feedback should occur before students leave school with their homework, during homework via technology, and after submitting homework. Feedback should come from students and parents about homework assignments and process, and it should inform future teaching and learning.

Feedback from students before they leave school should occur as they communicate their understanding of expectations before the homework is assigned. Timely deliberate homework feedback happens during the learning process so students are practicing correctly, specifies areas the student can improve, and/or asks questions. Feedback during the homework process can be aided by technology to help students immediately understand what they answered correctly or incorrectly and provide assistance as needed. Technology can be leveraged to enhance personalized homework feedback that happens immediately, explains mistakes, celebrates progress, empowers reflection, and inspires learning.

Feedback partway through the learning process can assist with understanding errors, misconceptions, accuracy, and depth as well as empowering self-help and self-assessment. Teachers can leverage technology to provide feedback during the homework process to alert a student about an incorrect answer. Support options can vary: students could select a different answer, or the correct answer could be displayed with an explanation of why it is correct.

If homework is related to upcoming learning, then performance should be reviewed in class and feedback should be provided after submitting homework and before proceeding with learning. Teachers can also provide feedback on work that students identify as their best to involve them in the decision process and to decrease the amount of work on which feedback is provided. Feedback after submitting homework can come from the teacher. However, peer feedback can be beneficial if structures are in place to guide the participation and feedback process. For example, students can discuss homework so they can explain what they learned or any mistakes they made. Self-evaluation can provide feedback when teachers provide correct answers so that students can check their own answers or explain their thinking, justify their answers, communicate potential changes in thinking or actions, or explain how they can improve.

Feedback from students and parents about homework assignments and processes should happen via teachers asking students to provide feedback about learning in the classroom every few months. Student feedback to teachers includes information about their understanding and thinking before homework is assigned as well as teachers using information from homework to inform future teaching and learning. Feedback from homework should also inform teaching, learning, and readiness for assessments. Homework should provide feedback to the teacher to help diagnose why a mistake happened or where the learning gap is. The teacher should then provide feedback to the student to close the perceived gap. Feedback also happens when teachers consider the feedback students are communicating when they don't turn in homework or there are multiple homework mistakes. Figure 10.1 is a reminder that students should provide feedback that guides future teaching. A great question is: What did you learn from your students that changed your teaching? Related research about deliberate homework feedback includes grading and assessment.

What did you learn this week about your students that changed your teaching?

Figure 10.1 What Did You Learn from Your Students?

Table 10.2 Guiding Primary Questions Regarding Homework Feedback

Guiding Primary Question	Your Response
How can you enhance timely feedback to help students achieve higher expectations?	
How do students act on teacher feedback about homework and how do teachers act on feedback they gather from homework?	
What changes can you make to ensure students receive feedback on most written work via a teacher, classmate, or self-reflection?	

The following implementation planner and reflection questions can guide discussions and potential homework improvements for feedback.

Table 10.3 Chapter Implementation Planner for Homework Feedback

Topics I will ...	Responses
Investigate	
Discuss	
Reflect on	
Change	

D.E.L.I.B.E.R.A.T.E. Continuous Improvement Questions for Homework Feedback

The following D.E.L.I.B.E.R.A.T.E questions can guide reflection, discussion, and professional learning by asking you to Differentiate, Explain, Learn, Implement, Bolster, Empower, Reflect, Ask, Terminate, and Entrust.

◆ *Differentiate*: How will you provide differentiated feedback that informs teaching and learning?

Differentiated feedback

Step 1. How will you maximize the use of information gathered while reviewing homework to provide differentiated feedback that informs teaching and learning?

Step 2. Discuss response with colleagues.

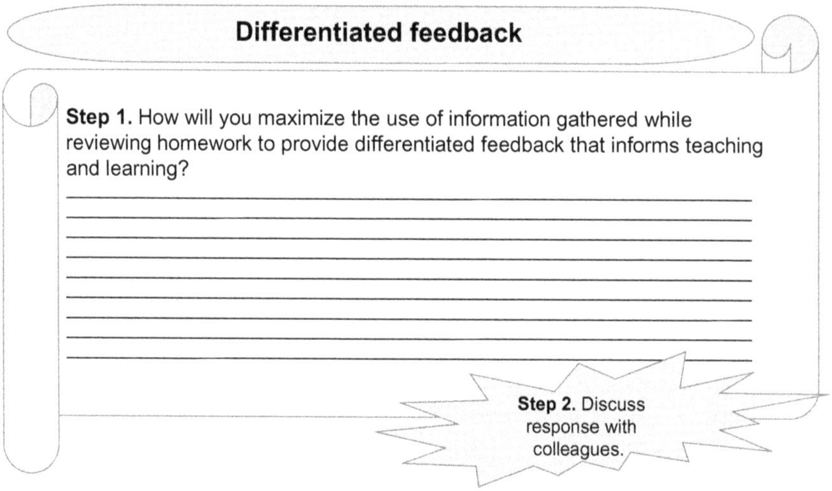

Figure 10.2 Differentiated Feedback

◆ *Explain*: Explain how you plan to provide students with actionable, specific, and timely feedback on homework rather than a grade.

Actionable, specific and timely feedback empowers reflection and improvement more efficiently than grades.

Figure 10.3 Actionable Feedback

◆ *Learn* more about providing feedback that empowers reflection and passion for learning, based on clear and understandable criteria and recent evidence. How will you track how students act on your feedback to better understand how effective your feedback was?

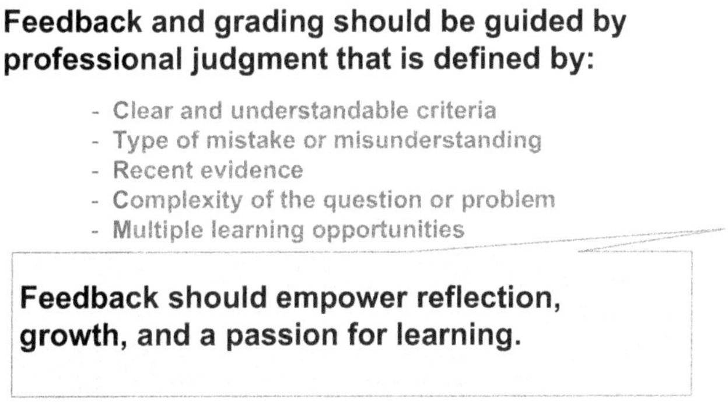

Feedback and grading should be guided by professional judgment that is defined by:

- Clear and understandable criteria
- Type of mistake or misunderstanding
- Recent evidence
- Complexity of the question or problem
- Multiple learning opportunities

Feedback should empower reflection, growth, and a passion for learning.

Figure 10.4 Feedback Based on Professional Judgment

◆ *Implement*: Explain how you will enhance feedback about homework.

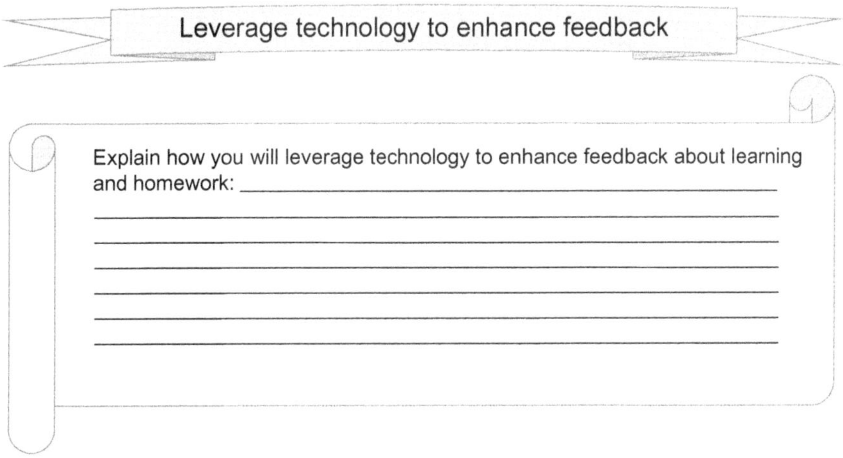

Leverage technology to enhance feedback

Explain how you will leverage technology to enhance feedback about learning and homework: _____

Figure 10.5 Leverage Technology to Enhance Feedback

◆ *Bolster* feedback by discussing with colleagues how to leverage technology to enhance homework feedback.

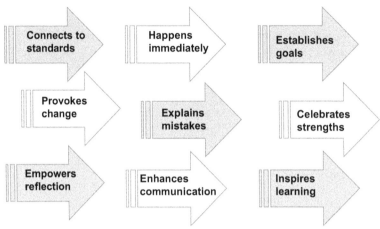

Figure 10.6 Leverage Technology to Enhance Homework Feedback

◆ *Empower*: What praise, questions, and guidance will your feedback include to empower student growth, reflection, ownership, innovation, and tenacity?

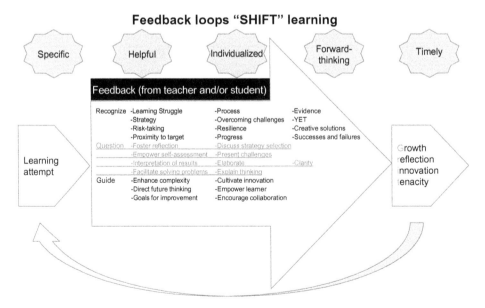

Figure 10.7 Feedback Loops Shift Learning

◆ *Reflect* on how timely and purposeful your homework feedback is as well as the extent to which it empowers reflection and change.

Effective teachers, coaches, and leaders provide timely and purposeful feedback that empowers reflection and change.

Figure 10.8 Timely and Purposeful Feedback

◆ *Ask* questions to empower reflection about independent practice: Explain a skill, strategy, or process that was effective for you. Explain a difficulty you had and potential solutions, strategies, or questions.

Questions to empower reflection about independent practice

Name: _____   Date: _____

Please review the following assignment and answer the questions below to empower reflection and improvement: _____

1. Explain a skill, strategy or process that was effective for you: _____
_____
_____
2. Explain a difficulty you had and potential solutions, strategies or questions: _____
_____
_____
_____

Figure 10.9 Questions to Empower Reflection about Independent Practice

◆ *Terminate* providing feedback only after learning and assessment occurs. Instead explain how you will ensure homework feedback is provided during the learning process to empower improvement.

Feedback

Provide timely and specific feedback
during the learning process rather
than only at the end of the learning
process when attempts are graded
and feedback is less useful and not
actionable.

Figure 10.10 Feedback

◆ *Entrust*: Explain how you will entrust students to persist while continuously reflecting on feedback and recalibrating perspectives, strategies, and goals.

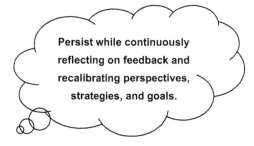

Figure 10.11 Persist while Reflecting

11

Grading Criteria

Grading feedback should be based on and align with learning targets, success criteria, and fair and accurate grading practices. Homework should only be graded as a behavior, such as responsibility, rather than as part of the overall grade for a subject, such as math. However, timely graded homework can communicate trends and provide feedback regarding mistakes as they relate to learning standards or skills. Before reading this chapter, please take a few minutes to answer the self-assessment statements below.

Table 11.1 Self-Assessment of Current Homework Practices

	Never	Rarely	Sometimes	Often	Always
My homework grades specify the number of correct and incorrect answers for each learning standard or skill so that trends can emerge.					
Success criteria and/or exemplars guide my homework evaluation.					

What

Deliberate homework grades should accurately reflect student proficiency regarding learning standards, should align with a common grading purpose, and should empower self-assessment. Teachers should review, grade, and provide feedback on homework with the purpose of understanding what additional practices and supports are needed. Deliberate homework criteria relates back to previously discussed characteristics of complexity, learning sequence, learning target, and communication. Deliberate homework grading follows eight distinct steps:

1. Count as a behavior grade such as responsibility.
2. Define by learning targets, success criteria, or exemplars.
3. Specify the number of correct and incorrect answers for each learning standard or skill so trends can emerge.
4. Record and track the complexity of questions for incorrect answers in the grade book to better understand student errors.
5. Allow for corrections on all homework to empower reflection and continuous improvement.
6. Empower analysis of the most common mistakes to guide teaching for class, small groups, or individual students.
7. Guide monthly academic or behavior goals that students create and track their own progress.
8. Mark unfinished homework as incomplete (I) and guide additional discussions to distinguish between chronic and infrequent homework completion problems.

Lack of homework support should not result in a low overall grade; instead it should be fed back to the teacher that additional student supports are needed. Thoughtless homework grading criteria are unfair, punitive, inconsistent, and/or not consistently understood by students and parents. Thoughtless homework grading criteria should not combine performance for tests, homework, and participation into one grade. Homework grades should not disproportionately negatively impact an overall grade. For example, a student who is missing three homework assignments should have a lower grade for behavior, such as responsibility, rather than an overall math grade of C. This low grade for responsibility more accurately identifies and communicates the area the student is struggling with rather than the student and parent seeing an overall low grade for the subject and not knowing if the grade is based on three missing homework assignments or understanding of the specific grade-level standards or skills. Potential negative impacts of not being deliberate about grading criteria include being unaware of success criteria for standards and skills. Challenges teachers may encounter include inconsistency among teachers and focusing on learning and not grades.

Why

Benefits of deliberate grading criteria include defined and clear expectations and success criteria. Deliberate homework grading criteria should explain success criteria regarding how homework is graded and should communicate information to students and parents regarding proficiency with different learning standards and skills. Deliberate homework criteria should allow students multiple attempts to demonstrate proficiency to create a focus on learning rather than a grade.

Missing homework should not impact the overall subject grade that is meant to communicate students' understanding of specific learning standards rather than explaining what information like homework or tests were used to calculate the grade. Homework should be graded as a behavior, such as responsibility, so homework trends can be isolated from performance in class. A reason to justify this recommendation is that teachers don't know whose work is being graded. Homework could have been completed independently, with support from a different student, or by copying a classmate's answers.

How

A focus on teaching and learning rather than mere compliance should guide homework grading decisions. For example, how should you follow up with a student who does not turn in homework but understands the targeted skill, compared to the student who did not turn in the homework and does not understand the target at school? Similarly, what questions do you ask, when a student does not submit homework, to better understand what happened and to enable you to help as needed in the future?

Targeted, concise, and occasional homework makes timely grading more efficient. Limiting the amount of homework will also limit time needed to grade. Fair and accurate grading is based on what grading practices teachers do, and which are not punitive. Deliberate homework grading happens when success criteria are constructed with students to guide evaluation of proficiency for learning standards or skills. Grading guidelines, success criteria, exemplars, and routines make the process more efficient, transparent, fair, and efficient. Grading should happen as soon as possible so that teachers and students are able to understand student proficiency levels and then be able to guide subsequent support in view of perceived difficulties. Homework reviewed and/or graded at the beginning of the next lesson allows students to discuss and reflect on their understanding, misunderstanding, misconceptions, or next steps. Grading can be completed by the teacher, classmates, or by the student who completed the homework. An efficient and transparent process should include grades written on returned work, students being encouraged to review graded homework and bring it home in a timely manner, and grades available online for parents to review.

Deliberate homework learning/grading criteria are thoughtfully planned to specify general guidelines for the school year as well as specific grading criteria for specific assignments. The specific criteria can include information defining the number of points the assignment is worth or the number of different standards or criteria that will be assessed. Shared, clear, meaningful, and relevant success criteria are established by students and teachers. Deliberate homework learning/grading criteria are understood by students, teachers, and parents and are consistent among teachers in different grade levels within the school district.

Homework grades are documented as a behavior grade such as "responsibility" rather than graded as part of an overall academic grade for subjects such as math. Deliberate homework grades enhance accuracy and meaning by (1) emphasizing recent evidence rather than averaging scores, (2) marking missing work as incomplete rather than with a zero, (3) reporting separate grades for different standards and behaviors, and (4) modifying the complexity of questions for all students rather than offering extra credit. Deliberate homework grades distinguish between what students can't do compared to what they didn't do and between infrequent or chronic challenges submitting homework. An example is a general rubric used for all work or homework. The rubric describes expectations by listing criteria and levels of quality for different standards or skills. Additional rubric options include differentiated rubrics that explain success criteria for different student ability levels and choices or student-created rubrics that define learning criteria and guide self-assessment of work.

Table 11.2 Guiding Primary Question Regarding Homework Grading Criteria

Guiding Primary Question	Your Response
What steps will you need to take to be able to report grades and provide feedback for separate standards rather than an overall grade and report homework as a behavior separate from academic grades?	

Related topics for additional research about deliberate homework grading criteria include grading and assessment. The following implementation planner and reflection questions can guide discussions and potential homework improvements for grading criteria.

Table 11.3 Chapter Implementation Planner for Homework Grading Criteria

Topics I will ...	Responses
Investigate	
Discuss	
Reflect on	
Change	

D.E.L.I.B.E.R.A.T.E. Continuous Improvement Questions for Homework Grading Criteria

The following D.E.L.I.B.E.R.A.T.E questions can guide reflection, discussion, and professional learning by asking you to Differentiate, Explain, Learn, Implement, Bolster, Empower, Reflect, Ask, Terminate, and Entrust.

◆ *Differentiate*: How will you gather feedback about understanding of, and effectiveness of, your homework grading criteria so you can differentiate as needed?

Effectiveness of homework grading

Name: _____   Subject: _____   Date: _____

Step 1. How will you gather feedback about understanding of, and effectiveness of, your homework grading criteria so you can differentiate as needed?

_____
_____
_____
_____
_____
_____
_____
_____

Step 2. Discuss your response with colleagues.

Figure 11.1 Effectiveness of Homework Grading

◆ *Explain*: What steps will you need to take to be able to report grades and provide feedback for separate standards, rather than an overall grade, and report behaviors separate from academic grades?

> Report grades and provide
> feedback for separate
> standards rather than an
> overall grade and report
> behaviors separate from
> academic grades.

Figure 11.2 Separate Standards

◆ *Learn*: Reflect on positive and negative impacts your homework grading practices have on different types of students.

> **Rather than assigning a zero for
> incomplete work that negatively and
> disproportionately impacts students'
> grades on a 100-point scale, mark the
> missing assignment incomplete, no
> evidence yet or in progress and define a
> process for the incomplete work to be
> completed and graded. Ultimately, a
> behavior grade for responsibility can
> reflect a trend of unsubmitted work.**

Figure 11.3 Behavior Grade

◆ *Implement*: Create a plan specifying how you will enhance accuracy and meaning of homework grades by reporting homework as a behavior.

Enhance accuracy and meaning of grades by...

1. Emphasizing recent evidence rather than averaging scores.

2. Marking missing work as incomplete rather than a zero.

3. Reporting separate grades for different standards and behaviors.

4. Modifying complexity of questions for all students rather than offering extra credit.

Figure 11.4 Enhance Accuracy and Meaning of Grades

◆ *Bolster*: How will your homework grades reflect unknown variables such as students receiving help with homework from classmates, parents, siblings, and technology resources?

In the classroom, teachers can control multiple variables when providing opportunities for practice or when checking for understanding.

However, homework can be unfair and gathered evidence can be less useful, because the students who need help may not receive help at home and other students may submit answers from their classmates, parents, siblings, or a technology tool.

Figure 11.5 Less Useful Gathered Evidence

◆ *Empower*: What actions will you take to empower student discussions and focus on priority learning standards to guide focused teaching, learning, and feedback?

Regardless if you report grades on a traditional or standards-based report card, assignments and grade books should still specify priority learning standards to guide focused teaching, learning and feedback.

Figure 11.6 Specify Priority Learning Standards

◆ *Reflect*: Explain how your homework grading criteria empower ownership, accountability, communication, reflection, self-assessment, and/or goal setting.

Deliberate homework grades...

1. Count as a behavior grade such as responsibility.
2. Are defined by learning targets, success criteria, or exemplars.
3. Specify the number of correct and incorrect answers for each learning standard or skill so trends can emerge.
4. Record and track complexity of question for incorrect answers in the gradebook to better understand student errors.
5. Allow for corrections on all homework to empower reflection and continuous improvement.
6. Empower analysis of the most common mistakes to guide teaching for class, small groups or individual students.
7. Guide monthly academic or behavior goals that students create and track their own progress.
8. Mark unfinished homework as incomplete (I) and guide additional discussions to distinguish between chronic and infrequent homework completion problems.

Figure 11.7 Deliberate Homework Grades

◆ *Ask:* Create a feedback form for students and families to help you better understand why homework is missing and to guide differentiated supports and routines.

Rather than primarily focusing on holding students accountable and penalizing their grade for missing work, **first focus on WHY the work is missing, what supports or guidance the student may need, and what questions can guide student reflection to empower ownership, learning, and growth.**

Figure 11.8 Focus on Why the Work Is Missing

◆ *Terminate*: Compare expectations for homework and grading to terminate ineffective practices while also enhancing consistency and best practices.

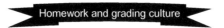

Reasonable that a student doesn't want to register for a class because the learning content is not meaningful, too difficult or the pace is too fast. Unreasonable that a student doesn't want to register for a class because of a perception that there will be too much homework or because the teacher is known as a difficult grader.

Figure 11.9 Homework and Grading Culture

◆ *Entrust*: What questions will you ask about consistent homework grading criteria?

Consistent homework grading criteria

Step 1. What questions will you ask to help determine if your school district has consistent homework grading criteria that align with best practices or recent research?

_____
_____
_____
_____
_____
_____
_____
_____

Step 2. Discuss response with colleagues.

Figure 11.10 Consistent Homework Grading Criteria

Information from the previous three chapters can collectively define whether your homework assignments are informative. Table 11.4 can be used to evaluate how informative any homework assignment is, based on the characteristics discussed in this book. You can evaluate homework by writing a checkmark under reasonable or unreasonable for each criteria. Modifications for some or all students include differentiating, enhancing, decreasing, or not assigning parts or all of the homework.

Table 11.4 Informative Homework Criteria

	Criteria	**Reasonable**	**Unreasonable**
Communication	I verified that my students could confidently understand and explain the homework directions and purpose in a way that was ...		
	I gathered feedback from parents and students about my homework communication to inform potential improvement in a way that was ...		
	I differentiated homework communication based on the varying needs of the students and their parents in a way that was ...		

(Continued)

Table 11.4 Continued

	Criteria	Reasonable	Unreasonable
Feedback	I wrote timely homework feedback in a way that was ...		
	I connected homework feedback with success criteria in a way that was ...		
	I gathered feedback while reviewing homework to inform future teaching in a way that was ...		
	I empowered students to act on teacher feedback about the homework, and I acted on feedback I gathered from the homework in a way that was ...		
	I ensured students received feedback on most written work via a teacher, classmate, or self-reflection in a way that was ...		
Grading	My homework grades specify the number of correct and incorrect answers for each learning standard or skill so that trends can emerge in a way that is ...		
	Success criteria and/or exemplars guide my homework evaluation in a way that is ...		
	Steps were taken to report grades and provide feedback for separate standards, rather than an overall grade, and report homework as a behavior separate from academic grades in a way that was ...		

IV

Consistent Homework

Deliberate homework should be reasonable, meaningful, informative, and consistent.

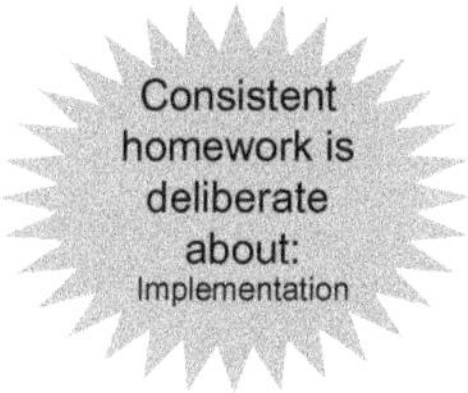

Consistent
homework is
deliberate
about:
Implementation

Figure S.4 Consistent homework is deliberate about

12

Implementation

Reasonable, meaningful, and informative homework are aspects of deliberate homework enhanced with consistent implementation that connects all of the features and explains recommendations for reviewing and creating consistent homework belief statements and practices. Implementation is defined as a process that includes communication, collaboration, planning, listening to feedback, and executing a homework plan in a classroom, school, or school district. Educators within the same school district and school should have consistent homework practices. Consistency makes it easier for students, teachers, and parents. If homework is not defined then, by default, school administrators are allowing teachers to define it individually. Before reading this chapter, please take a few minutes to answer the self-assessment statements below.

Table 12.1 Self-Assessment of Current Homework Practices

	Never	Rarely	Sometimes	Often	Always
My assigned homework is consistent with other teachers in my grade level, school, and school district.					
The teachers in my grade level, school, and school district have shared homework beliefs.					

What

Consistent homework expectations among teachers in the same grade level, school, and school district are beneficial for students and parents. Consistency of homework practices can be created with a common language that could include belief statements or responsibilities for students, teachers, and parents. Consistent homework implementation is a collaborative process that builds on shared needs and results in reasonable, meaningful, informative, and consistent homework practices and expectations.

Careless implementation lacks planning, collaboration, focus, consistency, support, and execution. Negative effects of inconsistency are enhanced when multiple characteristics are involved. For example, frequency and completion time are common topics, but inconsistencies are magnified when characteristics such as complexity and grading criteria also negatively impact students and families.

Why

We must empower research, reflection, discussion, and collaboration to change from "This is the way we always did it" to "This is best for kids." A deliberate implementation is a collaborative process to define homework beliefs to make homework more reasonable, meaningful, informative, and consistent. A well-defined process empowers students, parents, and educators to collaboratively identify ideal outcomes as well as practices they no longer want to continue. Educators must recognize that change is difficult. However, a defined vision, deliberate plan, and supportive collaboration will make the change successful. Potential negative impacts when not deliberate about implementation include inconsistent expectations and practices. Without consistent implementation, teachers create their own expectations or grading criteria. Some teacher expectations may be too rigorous, while some may not be rigorous enough. Some grading criteria may be fair and accurate, while others are unfair and inaccurate.

How

Ask the correct question(s) at the correct time to the correct people and listen to responses so as to empower dynamic work, collaboration, growth, and change. Discuss why homework is an important topic by asking staff why teachers, students, and parents in a school district should have shared belief statements that guide the homework process. Answers to this question can create a common purpose and urgency for investing time in this important process when there are other topics and initiatives and only a finite amount of time. A deliberate implementation involves students, teachers, and parents in the problem solving process. Noted below are six steps of deliberate homework implementation:

1. Describe current practice;
2. Establish plan;
3. Gather and evaluate information;
4. Define goal and shared vision;
5. Create common language;
6. Review feedback, celebrate successes, and discuss potential changes.

Describing the current practice involves understanding general homework practices as well as thinking of questions that should be potentially investigated. A critical part of this process is recognizing and celebrating the effective teaching, learning, and homework characteristics in place. Establishing a plan includes defining the process, identifying committee participants and any guiding homework research, detailing communication plans, and identifying intended outcomes regarding goals, structures, and timelines. Planning is critical to ensure that feedback is created from all stakeholders so the created plan reflects perspectives and needs accordingly. Educators can gather information via committee meetings and surveys from students, teachers, and parents, and then evaluate data to prioritize the next steps. Teachers can define goals and a shared vision by creating urgency for deliberate homework, building capacity among staff, and defining general goals of the homework implementation. Creating common language empowers consistency, coherence, and a learning mindset. A common language could be homework belief statements or a list of responsibilities for teachers, students, and parents. The final document should be shared with students, teachers, and stakeholders. The final phase of the process is reviewing feedback, celebrating growth and successes, and discussing potential changes. The formal documents and homework practices can be annually reviewed in the spirit of continuous improvement.

Table 12.2 Guiding Primary Question Regarding Homework Implementation

Guiding Primary Question	Your Response
What belief statements guide consistent homework practices in your classroom, grade level, school, and school district?	

The following implementation planner and reflection questions can guide discussions and potential homework improvements for implementation.

Table 12.3 Chapter Implementation Planner for Homework Implementation

Topics I will ...	Responses
Investigate	
Discuss	
Reflect about	
Change	

D.E.L.I.B.E.R.A.T.E. Continuous Improvement Questions for Homework Implementation

The following D.E.L.I.B.E.R.A.T.E questions can guide reflection, discussion, and professional learning by asking you to Differentiate, Explain, Learn, Implement, Bolster, Empower, Reflect, Ask, Terminate, and Entrust.

◆ *Differentiate*: What changes would you make to differentiate a homework review process in your school district?

Deliberate homework implementation

1. Describe current practice
2. Establish plan
3. Gather and evaluate information
4. Define goal and shared vision
5. Create common language
6. Review feedback, celebrate successes, and discuss potential changes

Figure 12.1 Deliberate Homework Implementation

◆ *Explain* how consistent the daily homework expectations are in your grade level, team, department, school, or school district.

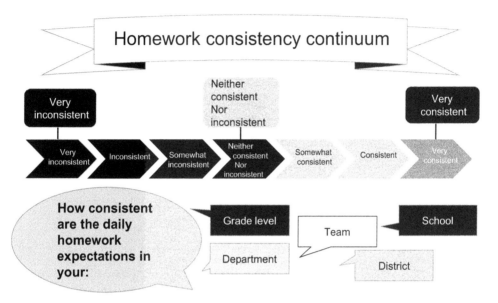

Figure 12.2 Homework Consistency Continuum

◆ *Learn*: Identify and commit to learning about as well as applying and sharing findings regarding creating district homework belief statements.

Sample homework beliefs (K-8)

Teachers believe meaningful homework should be connected to classroom teaching as a means to support and enhance learning. Homework should be timely independent practice of a targeted skill at the appropriate difficulty level. Homework should foster application, understanding, and proficiency while building students' academic success and confidence in the classroom. Homework should not be burdensome.

Homework is an opportunity to:
  - reflect upon (review, rehearse, and practice) material addressed in class.
  - allow for demonstration of self-direction, responsibility, and accountability.
  - communicate student learning with family.
  - take part in shared reading at home.

Figure 12.3 Homework Beliefs

◆ *Implement*: What reasonable and meaningful homework guidelines might work in your school district?

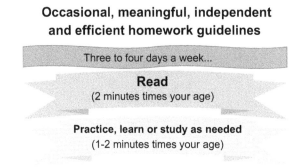

Figure 12.4 Three to Four Days a Week

◆ *Bolster*: How could you bolster this homework example to meet the needs of the students in your classroom, school, or school district?

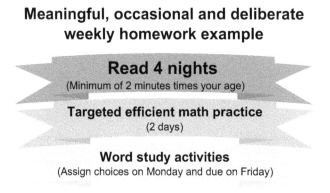

Figure 12.5 Read Four Nights

◆ *Empower*: How should your school district leadership empower student and teacher ownership during this homework implementation process?

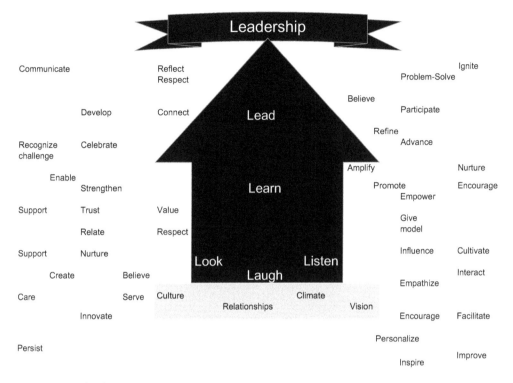

Figure 12.6 Leadership

◆ *Reflect* on how your typical homework impacts relationships between you and your students, your students and their parents, and you and your students' parents.

Ask questions and reflect to better understand how homework impacts relationships...

If and when you assign homework, reflect about how your typical homework impacts relationships between:
• **You and your students**
• **Your students and their parents**
• **You and your students' parents**

Figure 12.7 Impacts on Relationships

◆ *Ask* students questions to analyze homework.

Homework analysis

Step 1. Ask students to document the number of minutes they spend on homework for each subject every night for three weeks. Ask students to graph the results and compare the information to feedback collected via staff and parent surveys. Guided by collected data, write homework belief statements to guide general homework practices for your school district.

Step 2. Discuss response with colleagues.

Figure 12.8 Homework Analysis

◆ *Terminate*: What homework practices do you hope to terminate?

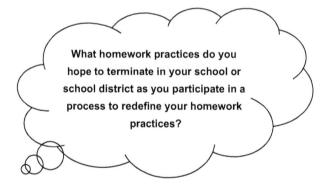

What homework practices do you hope to terminate in your school or school district as you participate in a process to redefine your homework practices?

Figure 12.9 Redefine Homework Practices

◆ *Entrust* teachers to discuss where their typical homework assignments would be classified on the homework spectrum below.

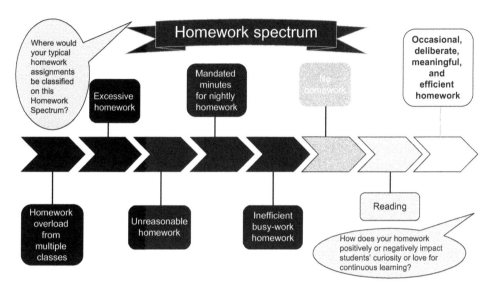

Figure 12.10 Homework Spectrum

Conclusion

This book does not discuss whether homework should or should not be assigned. Instead it empowers reflection on how to assign homework that is reasonable, meaningful, informative, and consistent. Rather than mandating or banning homework, educators should collaboratively scrutinize the 12 deliberate characteristics in this book to enhance learning opportunities to build on individual student strengths while supporting weaknesses. Homework practices should ultimately align with best practices for teaching and learning while also recognizing the unique dynamics of individual students, families and communities. Meaningful homework connects to priority learning standards to enhance focus and guide timely and actionable feedback that students and teachers deliberately act on. Revisiting the guiding questions from the Introduction empowers educators to apply a deliberate mindset about homework as they reflect on criteria that guide decisions for assigning homework. Responses to this reflection (see Table C.1) should be guided by the 12 characteristics of deliberate homework.

Table C.1 Guiding Primary Question Regarding Deliberate Homework

Guiding Primary Question	Your Response
What criteria guide decisions for assigning homework?	

Reasonable homework is created by focusing on the first three characteristics: (1) completion time, (2) complexity, and (3) frequency. Reasonable homework focuses on its frequency and the amount of time needed to complete it. Enhanced outcomes include established criteria, equity, ownership, and a broader definition of independent practice opportunities. The next five characteristics collectively explain why meaningful homework includes deliberate (4) purpose, (5) learning targets, (6) learning mindset, (7) format, and (8) sequence. Enhanced outcomes include ensuring that the format for every homework assignment has a meaningful purpose, appropriate complexity, and aligns with a pertinent learning target as well as positive impacts on student passion and curiosity for learning, alignment with learning targets, and trusting relationships that empower a learning mindset. Informative homework is created by focusing on the next three characteristics: (9) communication, (10) feedback, and (11) grading. Enhanced outcomes include students understanding homework purpose and directions and leveraging action after feedback to enhance proficiency on priority standards and skills. Finally, characteristic (12), deliberate implementation, connects all of the characteristics and explains a process for collaboratively creating homework belief statements that guide deliberate, reasonable, meaningful, informative, and consistent homework.

Reasonable, meaningful, informative, and consistent homework should be connected to classroom teaching as a means to support and enhance learning. Homework should foster application, understanding, and proficiency while building students' academic success and confidence in the classroom. Homework should not be burdensome. Deliberate homework opportunities should be independent practice of a targeted skill at the appropriate difficulty level rather than dependent on support from parents or others and should not interfere with time for family, extracurriculars, and community. Deliberate homework opportunities should ultimately engage, motivate, support, and challenge students and strengthen collaboration between schools and families.

The two guiding levers of frequency and amount of differentiation can guide changes for each of the 12 characteristics of deliberate homework. Guiding levers to enhance the impact of deliberate complexity include the frequency each week or month of modifications, flexibility, student choice, or student reflection about their learning. An example synthesis of the 12 characteristics results in deliberate homework that allows for multiple days to be completed, is differentiated, assigned only once or twice a week, is purposeful, and is aligned to learning targets. The deliberate homework empowers meaningful practice, creativity, connections, and/or reflection; it is meaningful and effective and includes understandable two-way communication. It is evaluated via fair and understandable grading criteria; includes concise and purposeful feedback that empowers improvement; aligns with a student's learning mindset that includes being responsible, resilient, reflective, resourceful, and receptive to feedback; and the homework is consistently and purposefully implemented.

Hopefully this book inspires reflection about the ways homework can be made more reasonable, meaningful, informative, and consistent to provide a positive impact on collaborative partnerships among educators, students, and families. The recommendations should guide school districts to empower a continuous learning mindset by collaboratively building a culture that recognizes student interactions with family and community outside of school while continuing to learn and unlearn how to inspire homework opportunities that deliberately practice, differentiate, communicate, explore, and innovate. The ideal outcome is that teachers are empowered to ask the correct homework questions at the correct time, seek feedback from parents and students throughout the process, and use the questions in this book to guide reflection, change, and continuous improvement.

Most days I tell my three daughters to be kind, curious, and creative. As a father I would prefer to discuss with my children what they are learning, who they were kind to, or what they are curious about, rather than my typical question of what do you have for homework. Homework may not always encourage students to be kind, curious, and creative; however, homework definitely should not discourage students from being kind, curious, and creative. Questions and responses from the self-assessments, chapter implementation planners, and guiding primary questions for each of the 12 characteristics should guide prioritization of characteristics, ongoing discussions, and reflection on deliberate homework improvements.

Table C.2 Deliberate Homework Change Process

Prioritize three homework characteristics that you could enhance. If unsure, starting with reasonable characteristics of completion time, complexity, and frequency are logical starting points.	1. 2. 3.
Establish goals that are specific, measurable, attainable, relevant, timely, inclusive, and equitable.	Specific: Measurable: Attainable: Relevant: Timely Inclusive: Equitable:
Explain how you will discuss with others and gather feedback.	
Reflect on gathered feedback and prioritize three changes:	1. 2. 3.
Prioritize three homework characteristics to enhance and begin the process again.	

The following implementation planner and guiding reflection questions from each chapter can guide ongoing discussions and reflection on deliberate homework improvements.

Table C.3 Book Implementation Planner for Homework Changes

	Guiding Primary Questions	
Reasonable	What criteria guide decisions for assigning homework?	
	How many minutes will it take to complete this homework assignment for the student who understands directions and concepts and has all of the resources? And how many minutes will it take for a student who does not understand the concept and may be missing some of the resources?	
	How much time do your students spend on homework for you and other teachers each week?	
	How can inequity of homework for certain students empower change related to how you provide independent practice for all students?	
	How will you empower a student to own his learning and enhance his understanding of his own capabilities and progress?	
	What changes would you need to make to help students benefit from a maximum of one night of weekly homework?	
	If you think of homework as practice, what practice opportunities can you provide in your classroom rather than as homework?	
Meaningful	How does your homework enhance or decrease students' passion for curiosity and learning?	
	How will you deliberately connect homework to classroom teaching as a means to support and enhance learning?	
	How can you enhance alignment between your homework assignments and effective learning targets and strategies?	

(Continued)

Table C.3 Continued

	Guiding Primary Questions	
	How will you model and empower a learning mindset to enhance focus on students being responsible, resilient, reflective, and resourceful?	
	How will you build trusting relationships and a culture that empowers courageous continuous learning with a growth mindset?	
	How can you ensure that the format for every homework assignment has a meaningful purpose, appropriate complexity, and aligns with a pertinent learning target?	
	What modifications need to be made regarding the sequence of homework questions on individual assignments as well as related assignments?	
Informative	How can you verify that your students can confidently understand and explain homework directions and purpose?	
	How can you enhance timely feedback to help students achieve higher expectations?	
	How do students act on teacher feedback about homework and how do teachers act on feedback they gather from homework?	
	What changes can you make to ensure students receive feedback on most written work via a teacher, classmate, or self-reflection?	
	What steps will you need to take to be able to report grades and provide feedback for separate standards, rather than an overall grade, and report homework as a behavior separate from academic grades?	
	What belief statements guide consistent homework practices in your classroom, grade level, school and school district?	

For Product Safety Concerns and Information please contact our EU representative GPSR@taylorandfrancis.com
Taylor & Francis Verlag GmbH, Kaufingerstraße 24, 80331 München, Germany

www.ingramcontent.com/pod-product-compliance
Ingram Content Group UK Ltd.
Pitfield, Milton Keynes, MK11 3LW, UK
UKHW031041080625
459435UK00013B/571